TIMBER FRAME

HOUSES

IN THE

SCOTTISH

COUNTRYSIDE

John and Margaret Richards

HMSO:EDINBURGH

First published 1994

© Crown copyright 1994

This publication is commissioned by The Scottish Office Building Directorate.

The authors acknowledge with gratitude the many helpful comments on the discussion document on which this publication is based, and the co-operation of all those who have given permission to illustrate their buildings and designs, and to make quotations from other publications.

The opinions in this report are those of the authors, expressed on behalf of John Richards Associates, and do not represent those of The Scottish Office.

Unless otherwise stated, all photographs are by the authors.

ISBN 0 11 495191 8

FOREWORD

As a result of the increasing pressures on our countryside, there is a widespread interest in maintaining the quality of our rural environment, and a growing awareness of the visual impact of new development in the countryside. In the White Paper "This Common Inheritance" the Government gave a particular commitment to the preparation of guidance on the location and design of rural housing in Scotland.

This report on the design of new housing in the Scottish countryside is a significant addition to the guidance available on design and rural planning issues and, as Minister with responsibility for housing, I am delighted by its publication. I am confident that the practical advice contained in the report will make a valuable contribution to the current debate on how to ensure that the location and design of rural housing is in keeping with the high quality of Scotland's landscape.

I commend this report to all those engaged in the procurement, design, approval and construction of new houses in the countryside.

Lord James Douglas-Hamilton MP
Minister for Housing
February 1994

CONTENTS

I

INTRODUCTION

The Scottish Office's Planning Advice Note 36, *Siting and Design of New Housing in the Countryside*, was published in 1991 to encourage planning authorities to give design guidance on houses appropriate to rural areas. PAN 36 (as it has come to be known) was written to be used mainly by the elected members and officials of planning authorities.

This publication, however, is aimed at a wider readership: house builders and component suppliers, house designers, and the general housebuilding public, as well as planners. It is based on research, commissioned by the Scottish Office Building Directorate in 1992, and carried out by the authors, assisted by Jill Andrews. The research report was published as a discussion document and circulated to consultees in the industry and the professions, and to planning authorities and amenity bodies. Many of these have since made valuable comments.

The study is concerned with a particular aspect of the subject of house design in the Scottish countryside: the design of houses which individuals provide for themselves, rather than those which are designed and built speculatively by developers. The study is focussed on houses built with timber frames. Many of the designs for these are derived from the brochures of suppliers of prefabricated timber frames. Such houses are usually called 'kit houses', although the use of this term has been restricted in this report to standard house designs in brochures and the houses built from them without significant modification. There has been widespread public criticism of some of the standard kit house designs when these are used in the countryside. One of the aims of this study has been to survey the range of standard designs on offer from timber frame suppliers and builders, as described in their brochures, and to assess whether these designs are suited to the rural environment.

The concept of individual provision, though not new, and though popular in many other countries, has not been widely applied in Scotland in this century. Generally speaking, new houses for owner occupation in urban and suburban areas have been bought ready built from speculative house builders. In rural areas, however, most new houses are developed by individuals for their own use, and this trend appears to be growing.

This trend has important effects on the way houses are designed. A noticeable recent change in the appearance of much of Scottish post-war housing is that few housing developments are now built to standard designs on a large scale. Housing has come out of uniform. This is especially true of individual provision. Individual providers developing houses for themselves can be expected to make design choices, and at times they will wish to be distinctive in the choices that they make. Design initiative has moved to the householder.

Most new individually provided houses in Scottish rural areas are timber framed. In these houses the structural walls and roofs, and the other joinery components, are normally prefabricated off site. Individuals providing houses for themselves can select standard house designs from brochures which have been prepared by suppliers of integrated systems of timber frames and joinery components to market their products, or have these designs modified. Alternatively they can have new designs prepared to suit their needs or tastes.

This study offers design guidance for the development of these houses in the Scottish countryside. It has been conducted largely by speaking to those who take part in the design, approval and building process. Where sample surveys have been undertaken these have been intended to give an indication of the influences of a particular issue, rather than to provide comprehensive data.

Timber framing is a method of constructing the superstructure of houses, not a closed design system, and many of this report's comments and recommendations on design apply also to masonry construction. Similarly, many of the design issues discussed in the context of individual provision apply equally to small scale rural developments by speculative and other house builders.

Although there is a strong case for planning authorities to prepare simple design guidance aimed at applicants for planning consent, this is not the purpose of this study, which is written for those who are prepared to go into the subject in greater depth. The subject is complex and a full discussion of principles is necessarily too wide-ranging to be reduced to a short set of simple rules. Conditions of climate, landscape character, materials and architectural tradition all vary widely across Scotland, and detailed guidance to applicants can be expected to vary from one authority to another. Local planning authorities, not consultants, are responsible for determining local planning policy. For all these reasons the recommendations which follow are not intended to be used as a substitute for local guidance, nor to be used selectively as a basis for prescriptive control.

The authors' approach has been to consider design quality as a whole, taking into account all relevant considerations. They have done so in the conviction that only by going beyond a superficial consideration of styles will it be possible to find policies for design guidance which can be put forward and explained convincingly.

'Beauty is the complexion of health. To reach it we must put aside our preoccupation with different sorts of rouge'. [1]

II

THE CUSTOMERS

Despite the growing policy interest in individual provision little systematic information on this type of housing is available. About 9% of total private development in Scotland is individual provision.[2] The proportion of individual provision is higher in rural areas, where it can be as high as 85% of new houses, although the variations between these areas is pronounced. In the remoter rural areas, where there is little speculative private sector development of new houses, there is a long tradition of individual provision.[3] This sector is thriving and growing. In the more remote rural areas, individually provided houses are for the most part relatively inexpensive, and are mostly developed by local people with limited means.[4] There are, however, significant exceptions in the more prosperous areas where there are commuting pressures. In some of these, the great majority of new rural households are commuters from major villages. and towns. In Moray, for example, only 1 in 20 of those occupying a new house is employed locally in the countryside. In the Borders, 70% of new sites are being developed by households relocating directly from urban areas, and 59% of new householders have at least one commuter employed outside the Borders region.[5]

The number of people aspiring to home ownership in rural areas exceeds the number who can realistically achieve it given present constraints on incomes and supply. The nature of the demand varies: commuter pressure in travel-to-work areas, second and holiday home pressures, and in-migrating settlement. The 1991 Census shows a population gain in most rural areas: the greatest percentage increases in the past ten years were in Highland and Grampian Regions. Constraints on supply include the limited availability of sites for individual house-building, servicing difficulties, and the higher costs of construction in rural areas. The result is that existing house prices and land prices are high, and local people find it hard to compete in the main rural areas. Within the owner occupation sector individual provision was the preference of 13% of those recently surveyed, but only 5% saw it as a realistic option.[6] There appears to be a large, but latent, further demand from locally employed residents which would be released if some of the supply constraints were to be eased, as an outcome of current rural housing policies.

Information on the design aspirations of the customers is scanty. In a recent survey, attitudes towards functional considerations, landscape, solar orientation and energy efficiency all seemed to have lower priority in new houses than did external views, internal floor space or cosmetic appeal. Concerns over the quality of the new-built environment in rural areas probably have more causes than could be resolved solely by design guidance. The attitudes and aspirations of the majority of new rural householders interviewed, and the guidance available from designers, showed a marked urban orientation with a tendency towards disregard of rural issues. In pressured commuting areas the survey showed predominantly urban-style dwellings, designed and built by predominantly urban-style designers and builders, for predominantly urban out-migrant commuting new rural dwellers.[7]

Discussions with the authors have suggested that in many cases design attitudes have been shaped by the suppliers' brochures. The suppliers of timber frame houses often claim that they supply what the market demands in terms of design. They argue that they are experienced in reading signals of consumer demand, and have a commercial incentive to read these signals accurately. But these arguments can be countered by the observations that what is on offer may not be the best standard of design available, and in particular is likely to be limited to the ranges most likely to sell to the largest market, which may not be the rural market: the consumers' choices will be limited to what is on offer

It is reasonable to suppose that the previous architectural experiences of householders, travel, television and magazine illustrations also all play a part in determining design attitudes. Planning applications reflect the design aspirations of the market, modified by expectations of what will be permitted. In at least some districts a design based on vernacular traditions is more likely to be chosen or commissioned by incomers, whereas a distinctively non-traditional house is more likely to be wanted by local people. These preferences possibly reflect differences in costs and personal resources, although it not always the case that designs based on vernacular traditions are dearer to build and maintain.

Some locally employed people aspire to houses different in style to those they have grown up in, as a sign of their greater prosperity and of their rising aspirations for comfort and convenience. In crofting districts there are signs of earlier vernacular traditions being rejected by customers and local councillors alike as reminders of a poverty ridden past. In the views of some commentators these preferences, though understandable, are regrettable: they should be balanced against a sense of collective pride in and respect for our traditions.

Fewer than half of new timber frame houses now being built by individual providers are standard brochure designs used without modification, and significant numbers of timber frame houses are purpose-designed, but in some remote areas until recently there were no low-cost alternatives to the standard DAFS (now The Scottish Office Agriculture and Fisheries Department) croft house or the standard kit designs.

III

THE SUPPLIERS

Timber frame, as a construction technique, is well established in Scotland. Timber frame construction accounts for almost one half of the output of housebuilders registered by the National House-Building Council (NHBC) in Scotland. 75% of house building by individual providers in the countryside (many of whom use non-registered builders, or who self-build) is by this method. The possibility of rising demand is significant if suppliers are to be convinced that it will be in their interests to invest in designs prepared specially for the rural market.

Timber frame suppliers claim that, to the occupier, a timber framed house offers low first cost and lower fuel costs because of the high insulation levels which can be achieved and, where occupation is intermittent, the low thermal capacity of the walls; to the designer, the timber frame method offers a flexible plan and relatively few constraints in the design of windows and other secondary elements, and in the choice of external claddings, finishes and details; and to the general contractor or self-builder, timber frame allows the house shell to be completed more quickly than with traditional masonry construction. Typically a house frame can be erected on a prepared base in a matter of days to provide a wind and weather-tight working site, allowing simultaneous working by separate trades contractors and subcontractors. These advantages are especially important in the Scottish climate. The structural components are lighter and more easily transported than traditional walling materials. These qualities are important in rural and island sites.

The durability of timber frame construction within the normal life-span of a house, if the work is properly detailed and supervised, is well established and has been confirmed by recent studies. The Building Research Establishment, which has studied 400 houses on 45 sites throughout the UK, has found that the risk of decay in the framing and sheathing of timber framed houses built in the last 10 to 15 years is very low. They regard the design and construction principles of this period as satisfactory, and consider that the guidance now available and improved practice in the construction of houses today should further reduce the risk of dampness and decay. The popularity of the method, which has been in use in Scotland since the 1930s, points to its suitability. NHBC's experience over the past 10-year period during which timber framed houses have been separately recorded is that they are relatively defect free and in terms of customer complaints these do not relate to the timber frame itself, but to the external masonry cladding, especially cracking to external rendering and distortion of windows. The latter usually results from insufficient allowance being made for the shrinkage of the timber relative to the masonry, causing, for example, the underside of windows to rest on the masonry and be subject to rotational movement.

Some commentators consider that there is too little redundancy in modern timber frame structures, which are calculated to minimum sizes for economy, and that this sets limits to durability and flexibility which they feel are too low. Even if this were so, these limitations would not be inherent in the method of construction, because timber components can be designed to be stronger if experience suggests that they should be. Wall and roof frames can be relatively economically designed to accommodate the greater thicknesses of insulation which may be required in the future to meet increasing standards of energy efficiency. All forms of construction can suffer from problems if the principles are not understood, either in the design office

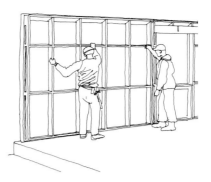

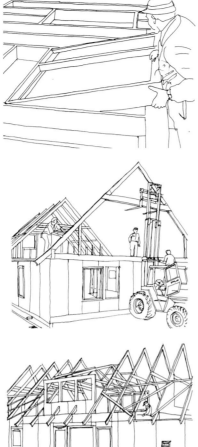

Timber frames are usually assembled in the factory, and delivered to the site with other joinery components. Wall panels are erected, windows installed, roof trusses lifted into place, dormers formed, and the interior completed within a weathertight shell.

or on the site. This applies to timber frame as to other methods of house building. Particular care must be taken with prefabricated timber structures that they are set out accurately, that alterations do not compromise the structural integrity of the construction, and that site operations follow the details and instructions provided by the designers and do not rely on past experience with other construction methods.

Modern timber frame construction in Scotland usually relies on off-site prefabrication of the structural elements. The members and frames for wall, floor and partition elements, and roof trusses, are cut to length and assembled off-site in factories. Frequently they are supplied as an integrated package together with other prefabricated timber components, such as insulation, stairs, windows, doors, and internal trim. This process is highly efficient and leads to production economies resulting in most cases to savings to superstructure costs.

It is a common misunderstanding that timber frame 'kits' are made up speculatively to standard designs, and that, as a consequence, the 'kits' themselves can not be altered. Almost invariably the frames and components are manufactured and assembled to order, and are easily adapted to non-standard designs. There is, however, an investment by manufacturers in design, and in the stocks of materials held, which is most economically recouped if the designs of the timber frame are not materially altered before production. The willingness of manufacturers to vary their designs to suit customers' requirements varies across the industry. Panel heights based on sheet sizes are usually standard to keep costs down. Some manufacturers purpose-design each house to the customer's requirements. Others are only willing to make small alterations to the frame but are open to any suggestion by the customer concerning the cladding, which they usually do not build themselves and in which they have little commercial interest.

Timber frames are currently supplied in Scotland by at least thirty different suppliers, including English and Scandinavian suppliers, and at least one Canadian supplier. The output of these firms is not restricted to individual providers: many of the firms also supply to speculative house-builders, and some do so on a large scale. There is no data on the proportion of timber frame output going to rural areas: it is a relatively small proportion for the major suppliers, whose main customers are speculative house-builders working in the suburbs. Other smaller suppliers operate entirely in rural areas. Typically these will buy-in the roof trusses, windows and external doors, but make the wall panels and other joinery components themselves, and either build the complete houses themselves or supply the joinery components to local builders.

Timber frame suppliers in Scotland are represented by a trade association, SCOTFI, which has twenty registered member firms and a number of supporting members. The industry is concerned at the bad publicity which the design of rural houses has received in the press recently. Manufacturers have said that they and their products are unfairly stigmatised, and that their designs reflect market preferences. Representatives of SCOTFI have said that their organisation is keen to co-operate with initiatives to improve design standards of houses in rural areas and the image of the product.

Speculative building is rare in the more remote rural areas because the restricted demand on the one hand, and the high unit costs associated with the problems of getting materials, labour and supervisory staff to the site, and the lack of economies of scale in building and infrastructure provision, on the other, make this form of supply unattractive to developers. Individual provision flourishes where speculative building does not, and vice-versa.

The structure of the building industry which erects houses in rural areas varies, according to location. In remote areas firms are generally small. For example, Skye recently had some eighteen building firms ranging from 2 to 20 men. The majority of these firms could only contract for one job at a time, with the construction of one house being their optimum job size. [8]

Some individual providers build all or parts of their houses themselves, and a high proportion manage the process of design and construction. Self-building and self-management can result in substantial cost savings. A recent survey of individual providers (not all of whom were building in rural areas) showed that only about one third of them had contracted out the construction on an all trades basis, and the remainder had employed individual craftsmen to carry out all or part of the work. 78% of the individual providers were involved in the management of the construction process. [9] Evidence taken by the authors shows wide variations from these averages, depending on locality. In one area nearly all customers of a timber frame supplier had contracted with him to build their houses for them on an all trades basis.

IV

DESIGN PRACTICE

DESIGNS IN BROCHURES

Suppliers of timber frame and joinery component packages almost invariably prepare brochures showing plans and illustrations of the appearance of standard designs for their houses, to market their products. Very few builders prepare brochures for houses to be built in load-bearing masonry for individual providers, because the need for standard designs in this type of construction is limited. The experience and qualifications of the designers of standard houses shown in brochures varies from firm to firm. Chartered architects are sometimes employed as consultants for the preparation of brochure designs, but are rarely employed in-house. In-house designers of brochure house types are usually architectural technicians with experience of the working methods of their employers. NHBC has a requirement for structural designs to be undertaken by an independent chartered engineer, and these requirements may be met at the brochure design stage. Most manufacturers use engineers experienced in this class of work, which normally extends beyond structure to include general construction, fire and sound insulation considerations. Illustrations of brochure designs are usually prepared by professional artists.

Some houses are built exactly to the designs in the brochures.

Because the main market for the larger timber frame suppliers lies in suburbs, few of them prepare special ranges for the countryside, but some medium-sized suppliers and smaller suppliers based in rural areas target their designs towards the rural market.

Timber frame suppliers, whether acting as main contractors, or as suppliers or subcontractors to builders, usually offer a design and management service to individual customers. Typically a customer will first approach the timber frame supplier and obtain a standard catalogue of plans and illustrations. From this point the supplier's design service can vary from very basic advice on the selection of a plan to the preparation of full tailor-made designs. At its simplest level, the customer discusses the most suitable plan with the supplier's representative, obtains a quotation for supply of the integrated package of timber components or the building of the house, and signs a preliminary contract to allow planning permission and building regulation approval to be applied for.

MODIFICATIONS

Alternatively the customer may treat the standard designs as a starting point for discussions with the supplier on layouts and appearance, obtain a quotation, and receive drawings of the modified design for planning approval. These more detailed designs are usually provided at no extra charge, although the supplier will have employed in-house design staff or have engaged an architect or design consultant, and an engineer, to make the modifications.

In some instances the customer will ask the timber frame supplier to make substantial changes, or to prepare a bespoke design, using his system as a basis. Usually the costs of the in-house design staff, or of the external architect or design consultant, and engineer, will be passed on to the customer. An in-house designer employed for these services will sometimes be a technician, with or without formal design training. External consultant building designers employed by the timber frame supplier are usually architects or design consultants, and engineers, experienced in the field of house design who have a close working relationship with the supplier. No survey has been attempted by the authors of the level of charges made for services provided by such in-house staff or consultants to timber frame suppliers to prepare client designs and modifications.

In a minority of cases the customer will first approach an independent architect or building designer, and possibly an independent engineer and quantity surveyor, who will give preliminary advice on design and may organise competition between timber frame suppliers before detailed design work begins. These services are charged for. In some areas surveyors and other agents advise on the choice of suppliers and builders. Independent advice at the early stages of the project allows the choice of manufacturer and builder to be made on the basis of design suitability, quality and price competition. A design may be prepared to a preliminary stage before the timber frame supplier is selected. Once the supplier is selected the consultants may be retained to make modifications to one of the supplier's standard designs.

TECHNICAL DESIGN

Because the design of the structural and other joinery is closely related to the manufacturer's production processes and standards, detailed technical design after the preliminary stages is normally carried out in close collaboration with, or by, the selected manufacturer.

In summary, there are three stages in the design process to be gone through when timber frame and joinery component systems are used:

- the brochure design stage,
- the client design stage, and
- the detailed technical design stage.

Design at each or all of of these stages may be carried out by the timber frame supplier's in-house staff, or by consultants employed by the supplier. Design in the last two stages may alternatively be carried out by consultants independently retained by the client.

TRADITIONAL ON-SITE FRAMING

It is not necessary for an individual developer to purchase his timber frame from a timber frame system supplier. In some cases individuals will prefer to commission consultants to prepare original designs for their houses, and order the joinery to be made up in the traditional way. Often the local joiner will do the work. Roof trusses may be made up on the site, or the roof built from cut rafters and purlins. Wall frames may be built using either on-site balloon frame or platform frame techniques. These procedures can give even greater design flexibility than is obtained by modifying a standard timber frame system. Internal volumes can be opened up and used more

imaginatively than is easily possible using the standard platform frame technique. There may be a price penalty to be paid for entirely one-off design and on-site construction by comparison with the more usual methods, but this is not always the case. Some clients prefer to create the maximum amount of local employment.

A typical timber system house from a national supplier, under construction before the addition of external cladding. The walls are protected by breather paper. At this stage the shell is wind and water tight.

Designers: Wellgrove Timber Systems Ltd.

DESIGN PROCUREMENT

The views of mortgage lenders can influence the arrangements entered into for supervision of the construction. Where houses are self-built or built by builders not registered with NHBC, lenders usually require architects or qualified surveyors with appropriate insurance to carry out periodic inspections during specified construction stages.

A limited response to a postal survey of suppliers undertaken by the authors showed that on average about three quarters of timber frame designs had been altered significantly by customers or designed from scratch. Within this average there were wide variations, confirmed by discussions with suppliers and planning officials of different Districts. One supplier based in a rural area in the west estimated that 20% of his output was built from brochure designs unmodified, 60% was modifed, and 20% was designed from first principles. Research by others has shown that 27% of timber frame house customers made alterations to the brochure design, in almost all cases in collaboration with an architect, and a further 40% had their houses designed from scratch, to meet their own needs, to fit into planning requirements, or to meet particular site requirements.[10] These conclusions from various sources indicate that some 67% to 80% of timber framed houses are modified significantly from the brochure designs or redesigned from first principles.

A house of similar size nearing completion. In this case the client commissioned an architect to prepare a one-off design. The timber frame was prefabricated and erected by a local joiner.

Architect: Frank Burstow of the Hurd Rolland Partnership, Kyle of Lochalsh.

A survey undertaken by the Royal Incorporation of Architects in Scotland has shown that of those architectural practices with a current interest in timber frame house design, two-thirds say that they would be prepared to offer a design service to outline design stage for less than £500. About three-quarters would offer more detailed work to scheme design stage for under £1000.[11] Some non-architect design consultants offer an effective design service, especially when they are familiar with timber frame house design. No survey has been made of their fees.

V

BUILDING ECONOMICS

The cost of building houses in the countryside can be much higher than in areas closer to urban centres. Indicative costs for Lochaber, Skye & Lochalsh and Argyll & Bute (excluding their island areas) vary from 105% to 115% of the average, while those for Orkney, the Western Isles and the Shetland Isles vary from 120% to 135% of the average. There are some Highland areas where costs are 140% of average indicative cost levels.

Reliable comparisons of the cost of timber frame construction with masonry construction are scarce, because comparative estimates of the costs of otherwise identical designs need to be made to reach conclusions for particular locations. The authors have seen estimates of reductions in cost by direct comparison with masonry construction which vary between 3.5% (in East Lothian) and 15% (in Argyll). Savings in the order of 10% are frequently claimed. It appears that while the use of prefabricated timber framed panels and roofs, and other components, usually leads to cost savings, especially at the lower end of the cost range, this is not universally true. In a recent study of new house building costs in the Borders, apart from construction time considerations (not costed), no significant price advantage was found to have been consistently attributable to either traditional or timber frame construction. Where clients and their designers actively sought more than three or four full competitive quotations, the final price showed significant cost savings.[12] In an example considered in Skye, a comparison of the costs of an attic roof based on cut rafters and gang-nailed trusses favoured the cut rafter solution. The overall package nature of the timber frame method can be an advantage in remote rural areas where there are problems of co-ordinating the delivery of a diverse collection of materials and components. Individual providers save on a number of administrative, marketing and financing costs which have to be met by speculative developers. Further substantial savings can be made by individual providers if they self-build or self-manage the process. In a recent survey, nearly all individual providers estimated the current value of their houses to be more than the total cost of provision by a considerable margin.[13]

Unsatisfied aspirations for new housing in rural areas outstrip supply. This problem is part of a wider economic and community regeneration problem in particular areas. Affordability is crucial if supply and demand conflicts are to be resolved. In many rural areas locally employed peoples' incomes are well below the national average. Among the solutions needing encouragement is the individual provision of affordable homes. Since 1992 Scottish Homes has offered individual grants for home ownership in rural priority areas. It will be important, in the context of national housing policy, that requirements for improved design do not price houses out of the reach of the people who need them.

Taking all technical and economic factors in combination, it is clear that individual provision, using timber frame houses, will remain a popular option for the forseeable future for those seeking new houses in the Scottish countryside. Timber frame houses have a particularly important potential for low cost rural housing. This potential has not so far been fully realised, largely because of lack of good design advice.

There are practical difficulties in gathering statistical evidence that good design improves the resale value of a house or saves the vendor marketing costs, because comparisons would need to be made between differently designed houses in otherwise identical circumstances. A telephone survey by the study team of a limited sample of estate agents and surveyors has shown that they all considered that, if the guidance in PAN 36 was followed, the houses would have a higher value than they would have had otherwise, but they were not able to quantify the difference. Some surveyors emphasised the importance of good siting and first impressions on approach. It is reasonable to assume that good design improves re-sale value and saves marketing costs

Some of the recommendations which follow in this report - for example that more investment should be made in good design by suppliers, and also by customers in adapting standard brochure designs to individual sites and requirements, that roofs of single storey houses should be pitched more steeply, and that details should be considered more carefully - would add slightly to costs. Some of the recommendations - for example that house forms are kept simple, that site excavation is minimised, that most windows are kept smaller, and that feature panels of more expensive materials on the elevations are avoided - would save costs.

The extra cost to the roof itself of increasing the roof pitch from 25 degrees to 35 degrees in a house of 93 sq. m. is only some £140, but to this must be added the cost of the additional heights of gables: the overall extra cost can be in the order of £1,200 to £2,000. Above a pitch of 35 degrees the costs, including the costs of the trusses, rise sharply, and once the roof pitch reaches 45 degrees the extra cost is best exploited by using attic trusses and gaining attic rooms. A 45 degree roof costs, for the same roof area, about three times the cost of a 30 degree roof. The extra cost of a roof at this pitch can be offset to a large extent by savings in other elements if an attic type plan is used to reduce the footprint area of the house. The extra costs of steeper pitches are greatest if the plan is deep and the trusses have to be split to allow them to be transported by road. Attic trusses suitable for one and three quarters storey construction are available. Many prefabricated attic trusses need a crane: this adds further to their costs in remote areas, in which purlin-type attic roof construction, or cut rafters built in-situ, may be more appropriate.

Given a level site on good ground a simple bungalow is usually the cheapest way to build a small house. For a larger house, a carefully designed one and a half or one and three quarters storey house can be cheaper than the single storey alternative with the same floor area on a more difficult site. Where an expensive roof covering is called for, a near-square two storey structure can be economical, but looks unattractive if it has a small floor area. Acceptable proportions for a fairly small two storey house are much easier to achieve with attic construction. In these, the plan depth, in relation to roof truss pitch and weight, and to staircase design, is critical to costs. Terrace houses and semi-detached houses are more economical than their detached equivalents.

Illustrations at the end of this report compare three houses of the same floor area with different configurations and features on similarly sloping sites. A basic bungalow of poor design and a shallow roof is compared with one with improved proportions and composition, and with an attic type house designed to minimise its impact on a sensitive setting. The building costs of all three types of houses, excluding their garages and site excavation costs, are almost the same. The extra costs of improving the appearance of the garages, and the reduced site excavation costs, of the two improved types have the effect of making the overall costs of all three design options also fairly similar. These costs are notional, and are based on an average of costings estimated in East Lothian and in Argyll, because the prices for some elements vary widely from one part of the country to another. Because of these variations, intending developers should obtain quotations for particular proposals before deciding between alternative design approaches.

It is likely that the net outcome of following the recommendations in this report, taking costs and resale value together, would bring a financial benefit to the customer. This could only be established by experience. There is a case for the promotion of a number of demonstration projects to prove the point.

VI

THE NOTION OF
THE COUNTRYSIDE

The notion that experience of the countryside offers a sense of the realities of nature, is not new. *'The physical nature of the universe is governed by law, not by caprice'* (Newton's Principia, 1687). Nor is the notion that nature's genuine order offers beauty. For eighteenth century philosophers and Victorian poets nature was not only beautiful; it was morally healing.

What do we want from the countryside today?

For city dwellers it is a place of escape. Experiences unobtainable in cities - the sweep of distant landscapes, pure air, smells of woodsmoke and flowers, the feel of the wind and the sound of running water - give balance to the artificialities of city life. It is also a place in which confidence can be restored. Over large tracts of Scotland the land has been shaped from stone, not malleable clay, and its character is the character of the people. Values which have established themselves in stable communities over the centuries to counteract remoteness and the power of the elements still hold good: interdependence, courtesy, good-neighbourliness. The need to fashion an existence from a hard natural environment has bred a respect for practical and time-tested solutions to problems, and a disdain for fashion. The architecture of the countryside is - reassuringly - an architecture of necessity.

For those who earn their living in the countryside, it is a place of work. It can also be the place of their forebears, the very ground in which their histories are rooted. To them the countryside is more than a leisure resource to restore the jaded spirits of city dwellers, notwithstanding the economic advantages of tourism and recreation.

Farm buildings on Skye.

Croft at Glenelg.

For planners and architects *'there is a feeling that while society may have devoured our towns (for which they have held us to be the scapegoats), they shall not, by God, devour our countryside.'*[14]

For all of us, large parts of the natural landscape and built environment in the countryside are outstandingly beautiful, our inheritance and legacy.

At a more practical level, there are economic arguments for conserving these assets. The Scottish Tourist Board tells us that Scotland's scenery and built environment is one of its primary attractions, quoted by 82% of visitors as the the feature they most like about Scotland. Regional planning authorities tell us that improvement in design should result in a more positive and flexible approach to housing development in the countryside, which could then make a greater contribution to the rural economy, and combat rural depopulation and disadvantage where this occurs.

The problem is that most rural areas are no longer populated mainly by those who earn their living from the land. Their numbers have been declining ever since the last war. Increasingly, the countryside has become a refuge for people who prefer to live out of the towns in which they work, and those who are retired. If it is to prosper, and if folk, work and place are be kept in balance, then it must be allowed to foster new sorts of small enterprise. Where there is an obvious functional connection between the house and agriculture or work-place, even the simplest small bungalow looks at home. But there is a distinction to be made between allowing opportunities for local work (and for housing those who have retired from it, or who are willing to fit in with its traditions and values), and the development of suburbia.

Suburbanisation offers neither town nor country, and diminishes the notion of both. *'It is the taming of the countryside into manageable plots, whose flora and fauna are equally reduced specimens of nature. Each house in its own plot with its own fence, its pavement and its orange street light - its own pets fed on tinned pet food and warmed by centrally heated doggie blankets - bears as much resemblance to the natural countryside of Scotland as bonsai trees do to untamed nature. It is the stamp of man upon nature; and from one end of Scotland to the other, man has begun to diminish into suburbia what previously he had admired as greater than himself'.*[15]

VII

THE PLANNING AND BUILDING CONTROL SYSTEM

Planning policies in place for the last half century aimed at preventing uncontrolled rural sprawl - an end to ribbon development, with green belts around the major cities and a general presumption against development in the wider countryside unless required for agriculture or forestry - have had popular support, but some of the underlying conditions which prompted these controls have changed in recent years. The present arrangements for public utilities mean that new rural dwellers will bear many of the costs of dispersal. Rural services networks can be made more cost effective if more households use them. Public opinion is in favour of conserving the vitality of rural areas. Maximising agricultural output is no longer the national priority it once was: farm policy is now looking for the means of curtailing production and finding new uses for unwanted land. These changes are bringing about a reassessment of rural planning policy.

The Scottish Office National Planning Policy Guideline 3 on Land for Housing was published in July 1993 and reaffirms the policy on development in the countryside previously set out in SDD Circular 24/1985. Under NPPG3, development continues to be encouraged on suitable sites in existing settlements. Coalescence of settlements and ribbon development should continue to be avoided. Isolated development in the open countryside should be discouraged, unless there are particular circumstances identified in development plans. The Government recognises that such circumstances will arise and the NPPG sets out some examples, drawing attention to PAN36 on the siting of new housing in the countryside. The need to maintain the viability of rural communities in areas of dispersed settlement and depopulation has led planning authorities to show in their structure plans those areas where there can be a presumption in favour of single houses in the countryside, and large parts of the land area of Scotland are already covered by this kind of policy relaxation.

Suburban house types prominent against the skyline in open countryside.

The issue of affordable housing is one which currently concerns rural planning authorities at both elected member level and officer level, and NPPG3 deals with it at

some length, recognising that planning authorities may properly take account of the need for affordable housing when putting forward their structure and local plan policies. Land supply, important though it is to economic and social objectives, is not directly relevant to this study. It has an indirect bearing in that restrictions on land supply have the effect of raising costs and reducing demand, and this in turn inhibits suppliers of prefabricated timber frame houses from investing greater design and marketing effort into the rural market.

NPPG3 emphasises that the siting of new houses in the countryside will often be crucial: good design cannot always redeem the damage done by inappropriate siting. Greater attention should be given to landscape character, the local landform and pattern of vegetation. Conspicuous sites are to be avoided, especially where important public views are affected. New houses should respect the scale and character of traditional housing in the area. The NPPG requires planning authorities to address the issues of landscape impact and design to the extent necessary to protect the environment from detrimental development and to enhance environmental quality without dictating matters of taste. To guide developers, authorities are asked to use their local plans (and, where appropriate, planning briefs) to establish realistic objectives and criteria against which proposals for new housing can be assessed. Developers are asked to pay special attention to the shape, layout and form of development and its impact on the landscape, to the choice of materials with colours and textures which will complement development in the locality, and to the visual impact of new developments from major road and rail routes.

The Scottish Office's Planning Advice Note 36 notes that the main criticisms of new housing in the countryside include the use of extensive underbuilding, and the introduction of suburban house types, which, because of their shape, low roof pitch, overhanging eaves and verges, window proportions and general detailing including site layout, are out of character with traditional local styles. They include also criticism of the use of materials such as facing brick and some types of artificial stone which can look incongruous in a rural setting, particularly when used in the same building. PAN 36 urges greater sensitivity towards siting and design, and encourages planning authorities to identify those aspects of building design which are characteristic of the indigenous architectural form and indicate how they can be taken into account in new building. The aim of this policy is to maintain design coherence, based on regional character. It is clearly desirable, in order to make this possible, that planning authorities should analyse their local architectural heritage, and consider its implications for the future.

Some planning authorities are currently preparing design guidance or revising earlier editions. Several earlier design guides by planning authorities in Scotland, and one by the National Trust for Scotland, have been seen by the authors. Although they were generally simple and readable, and most contained some useful guidance on siting and form, few seemed to be adept at getting across points of principle. All contained advice and in some cases mandatory requirements on points of detail, biased towards traditional precedents for details such as skews, window margins and window types. There was widespread criticism by consultees of some of these design guides for being unduly restrictive by failing to take account of people's needs and building technique, and of local variations in character. In the course of interviews, the view was often expressed that there is a danger that planning guidance may take a mindlessly historicist, and blanket, approach to new development.

Some examples were quoted, in discussion with the authors, of planning officials interpreting historical precedent too narrowly in exercising development control. One official explained to the authors that, in the absence of any other generally accepted criteria for good design, his safest course of action if recommending refusal of consent was to base his criticism on failure to reflect the style of nearby buildings. On appeal he could give evidence based on drawings and photographs of the local vernacular. The tactic is understandable: the vernacular is measurable, and judgements based on it appear objective, even if the decision to match it is (in some circumstances) itself questionable.

From these discussions it appeared that in some rural Districts the elected members of local authorities disagree with their professional planning officials on the criteria being applied, which they see as too restrictive.

Some agents of timber frame suppliers submitting planning proposals on behalf of customers are salesmen earning commission on every house that they can sell. It can be in their interest not to alter the brochure designs. Given the poor standard of many of the proposals that planning authorities receive it is understandable that planners produce guidance which takes applicants and their agents back to basics. Recommendations follow in this report aimed at overcoming these difficulties.

Building regulations have very little effect on the appearance of houses. Space standards and minimum ceiling heights which formed part of earlier regulations are no longer mandatory, other than some minimum activity spaces which do not affect the exterior. Regulations for minimum glazed areas and ventilation areas of windows, and other requirements for safe window-cleaning and for protection from accidental impact, can affect window design but they allow latitude in expression. The ventilation of roof spaces affects the detailing of eaves, and can affect the appearance of slating or tiling.

Many completed rural houses, particularly timber frame houses on sloping sites, have underbuilding which results in flights of steps up to the front and back doors. This restricts access by the ambulant and wheelchair disabled, whether they are occupiers or visitors. If the access regulations were to be extended in the future to cover domestic dwellings this would have an impact on the siting, construction and appearance of new housing.

VIII

THE DESIGN BACKGROUND

HISTORY

The popular concept of the Scottish rural architectural heritage comes almost entirely from the houses built between the mid 18th century and the early 20th century.[16]

Before this period lairds lived in tower houses, and farmers and clergy lived in simple rectangular houses built of undressed stone with thatched roofs. Farm workers lived in primitive houses built of the materials immediately to hand: walled with wattle and clay, or turf and rough stone; windowless; roofed with undressed timber and thatch, and floored with earth or clay.

Single storey farm cottage in Angus.

The agrarian reforms of the second half of the 18th century introduced planned developments and new building types. In the Lowlands estate villages and farm towns were built with dressed stone walls and slate roofs. The new houses took three forms. The first basic type, and the one most frequently built, was a small narrow single-storey rectangular-plan cottage with low eaves. The second type had two floors, one of which was in the roof space. The rooms in the roof space were lit by dormer windows. The cottage either had its eaves at the same level as for a single-storey house, or its eaves level was about midway between the upper floor level and its ceiling. (In this report the former version is called a one and a half storey house, and the latter version a one and three quarters storey house). The plans of these latter houses were also rectangular with a depth slightly greater than in the single-storey types. The dormers of the one and a half storey house rose out of the roof plane, but the dormers of the one and three quarters storey house were in the vertical plane of the wall below, breaching the eaves, and giving this type a larger upper floor area. The

One and a half storey estate cottages near Comrie, in Perth and Kinross.

third type, the full two-storey house, was adopted from about 1750. The plan depth was often substantially deeper than in the cottages. Especially in the more prosperous areas these latter were the houses of the farmers and clergy.

Houses in the countryside were generally built on level ground or lying along the contours of sloping ground, with the front door on the lower side of the plan. In the

One and a half storey cottage with front gable at Spean Bridge, in Lochaber.

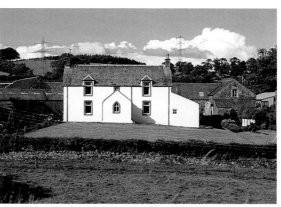

One and three quarters storey farmhouse at Powmill, in Perth and Kinross.

Two storey estate farmhouse near Glamis, in Angus.

Lowlands the later cottages were usually built in pairs or terraces adjacent to large farms. There are many variants of these basic types, including more elaborate detached estate cottages and lodges, often architect-designed, built in the mid or late 19th century on the more prosperous estates.

In the Lowland areas a range of regional styles developed in response to climate and geology from the mid 18th century onwards, against a background of a widespread adoption of a characteristically Scottish classical language of domestic forms and details.

The chief contributor to this language was the use of stone as a walling material. Stone was built as rubble, or was squared, or used as ashlar. In rubble work, windows and door openings, and the vertical corners of walls, needed a straight edge and extra strength which could only be obtained by using dressed stones as rybats. Corners, margins, and other embellishments added local character even in small houses. Stone walling relied on its thickness to carry loads, and, even if harled or limewashed, to resist the passage of water to the interior. The resulting character of stone walls in the rural heritage was one of massiveness and thickness. Although some individual early buildings were built of brick, and some parishes built fairly extensively in the material, the use of brick was not widespread prior to 1914.

In the east and south the stone was predominantly exposed. In the north and west it was traditionally lime-washed or rendered, although frequent examples can now be seen elsewhere. The origin of lime coatings and harling may lie in the poorer resistance of local stone in the west and the greater exposure to driven rain. It may also have been inspired by a need for brighter colour or as a response to larger scale landscapes in the west. Recently the use of white paint on walls or white dry-dash coatings has become more widespread.

Coloured finishes were traditional in some parts of Scotland. Usually these toned with the local earth colour. In Lothian, admixtures gave a warm orange colour to harling.

Traditional masonry in East Lothian. Whinstone rubble, with dressed sandstone rybats at window openings and the corners of walls.

Traditional roughcast with dressed sandstone window margins in the Borders.

In most areas the traditional roofing material was slate. Red and brown clay pantiles were traditional on the east coast and metal sheeting has a long history as a roofing material in the north. Roofs were symmetrically pitched. The average angle of the roof pitch varied between about 39 and 44 degrees, but significant numbers of roofs occurred above and below these slopes. Flatter pitches (from about 35 to 40 degrees) to roofs of single-storey cottages were more common in the south than in the north, where they tended to be steeper. Roofs were usually gabled. Chimneys were usually at the head of both gables.

Skews at the head of gables are characteristic in countries where buildings are of stone. By contrast, houses in timber-producing countries in areas such as North America and northern Europe have the roof running over the gable walls, sometimes producing large overhanging eaves and verges. Crowsteps are distinctively Scottish, but plain skews were much more common in the Scottish domestic vernacular. The width of the gable below the skew was thick when built of stone so that any water penetration was absorbed by the masonry. When skews were omitted the slates were usually sloped just beyond the ends of gables and tilted. It was usual for the slates to project some 25 mm (1") over any harling on the gable, and in traditional construction this was sufficient to protect the head of the harling from frost. Especially in the west and south-west, the slates were sometimes stopped just short of the verge against a raised lead or zinc fillet to prevent dislodgement.

In the majority of houses built across Scotland up to the end of the 19th century, especially in the north and west, and some Border areas, the eaves were closely trimmed: the gutter was fixed so that its inside lip lay close to the face of the wall and the slates projected by only some 25 mm (1"). A lintel, or an area of walling equivalent to the depth of the lintel, was normally visible above the window head below the eaves. The clear-cut geometry resulting from this detail and from skews or only slightly projecting slates at the head of gables is widely associated with the Scottish classical vernacular.

Large numbers of houses built in the late 19th century and early 20th century, however, combined masonry loadbearing walls with overhanging eaves and verges. These can be seen in both the Highlands and Lowlands but especially in areas of high rainfall and reasonable shelter from wind. The Victorian Gothic stylists introduced generously overhanging eaves with fascia boards and exposed rafter ends, often combined with overhanging verges and decorative timber framing at the gable. Projecting verges were often carried on purlins and false purlins used decoratively.

Scottish doors were traditionally broad and short, and either framed-and-lined or panelled. Rural builders did not emphasise the fanlight. Porches were commonly added to older houses in the north of the country from the 19th century onwards.

Up to 1914 almost all country windows were the sash-and-case type. This design suited the span of stone lintels and gave good protection against draughts and rain. The width of windows averaged some 850 mm (2' 9"). Consequently by far the majority of windows had vertical proportions. Dormer windows tended to be narrower. Country windows tended to be smaller than those in towns to allow the use of smaller panes, and perhaps also to give a greater sense of security from the weather. Several patterns of glazing division were used, the strengths of their popularity varying from region to region. In all cases the pattern was resolved clearly and restfully: that is to say sash transomes and mullions ran to the edges of the window, and astragals ran to the edges of the sash.

In some areas margins were used around windows to alter the scale, to soften the transition between wall and aperture, or to give emphasis. On rendered elevations margins were often painted, sometimes onto the rendering and sometimes onto flush or slightly projecting margins formed from stone rybats. Margins were hardly ever wider than 145 mm (5 ¾"). Nearly all traditional Scottish windows are set well back from the wall face, usually by some 150 mm (6"), with a tendency for a greater depth in the north.

Traditional small dormer, in this case rising out of the roof plane of an estate cottage at Airthrey, near Stirling.

Dormers were important in the Scottish tradition. Older (16th and 17th century) dormers were usually arranged to breach the eaves line. By the 18th century these became uncommon in cities, but in the country the use of wall-head dormers penetrating through the eaves persisted, although false dormers (above both the window head and eaves level) in the plane of the wall were not common until late Victorian builders revived them to add a palace-like flamboyance to their compositions.

The composition of the main elements of small buildings in most of the Scottish countryside, in the late 18th and 19th centuries, was often governed by overall proportional principles based on simple geometric ratios. It seems that the builders, working in an age when order and balance were valued, created well proportioned designs without effort.

Traditions along the west coast and in the Western Isles deserve special mention. The earliest permanent dwelling type was the blackhouse, a primitive structure with low, thick, dry-stane walls, a roughly oblong plan with rounded corners, a hipped thatched roof, and without daylight, ventilation or sanitation. Poverty slowed down progress to better standards. The earliest improved type, the whitehouse, had small windows allowing some daylight and ventilation, a chimney in the gable end, and lime mortar joints and lime render externally to improve the weathertightness of the walls. Animals were housed in a separate byre. Despite their many shortcomings, the whitehouses gave protection from wind noise and their directness of expression, and soft rounded outlines apparently growing out of the landscape, today leaves a potent image in the mind.

The need to improve housing conditions in these areas and to reduce depopulation led, in the late 19th century, to legislation and assistance. A new style of cottage evolved, originating from the pattern books and journals circulating at the time, symmetrical in plan, usually of one and three quarter story section. Walls were commonly about 600 mm (2 ft.) thick of roughly dressed stonework with mortar and render to improve resistance to horizontally driven rain. Corners, window and door reveals were squared off and gables were constructed with chimneys. Roofs were of slate or corrugated metal sheeting. Often small external porches gave protection to the door. Windows were deeply recessed, eaves were flush, and verges protected, usually by skews. These houses, many of which were built from the 1920s onwards, and which came to be called "improved cottages", have been in many cases ineligible for recent improvement grants, because their ceiling heights were too low, and have been abandoned.

Terrace on Skye.

Although sensitivity should be exercised in putting forward recommendations for such a fragile culture as that of Gaeldom, the "improved cottages" nevertheless seem highly relevant as a starting point in the search for a vernacular-based stylistic tradition to supercede the mediocrity of some recently popular kit designs in these areas.

The houses of the Scottish rural classical vernacular generally have clear geometric shapes. They are orderly, dignified and balanced. They look sturdy and strong.

Although their overall frontages are horizontal, this is counterbalanced by the verticality of their windows. Although some estate cottages and lodges have decorative and in some cases highly individualistic forms and details, as a general rule the style of the classical 18th century vernacular and its 19th century developments is ubiquitous and reticent. Unlike the buildings of countries with other traditions, most of the stone-based houses of Scotland give the effect of being dominated in their character by their walls, rather than by their roofs: walls appear massive and thick; eaves are often (though not always) kept close to the walls; dormers often penetrate through the eaves line in the plane of the wall; skewed gables often anchor the roof to the ground at each end.

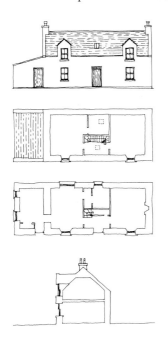

Improved cottage at Balemore, North Uist.

Revivals of the Scottish vernacular are not new. In the 1880s a second Scottish revival (the first had been based on picturesque romanticism) based itself on the accurate recording and measuring of buildings. The leading architects of the day - Robert Rowand Anderson, James MacLaren, Robert Lorimer and Charles Rennie Mackintosh - put forward a case for a practical, functional Scottish architecture, reflecting the rational planning and simple massing of the 17th century. The Arts and Crafts architects were lovers of the spirit of Gothic architecture - the Gothic of the craftsman - and were opposed in principle to classicism. In the cottage interiors and exteriors of such houses as Lorimer's Colinton houses, with their plain white walls, flowing spaces, and asymmetrical compositions, a new vernacular took root which abandoned the classical precedents of the 18th and 19th centuries.

This vernacular revival continued to flower between the wars and after the 1939-1945 war when Robert Hurd, Ian Lindsay, Frank Mears, and Basil Spence sensed that Scotland needed a new contemporary architecture. Frank Mears wrote in the RIBA Journal *'Buildings from the earliest to the latest, especially when they were faced with rough stone, harled and white washed, have a certain monolithic character; they are definitely cubic, if not cubist'*. A white, geometric, tradition based on vernacular forms was the basis for much post war domestic architecture, in both the private sector and the public sector. Alan Reiach and Robert Hurd, advocating a modern style for housing in an influential book written in 1944 illustrated examples of new, white, domestic architecture which were based on examples of harled work ranging from an 18th century house in Cromarty to Windyhill, in Kilmacolm, by Mackintosh. [17]

House at Torrin.

Vernacular revival cottage at Cairndow, in Argyll and Bute, by Ian Lindsay

Scots revival cottage at Colinton, in Edinburgh, by Sir Robert Lorimer, 1893.

Mid 20th century vernacular housing at Gifford by East Lothian County Council

Taken as a whole, the Scottish rural vernacular reflects the stabilising influence of a building technique which did not change materially for centuries, the slow evolution and refinement of craft traditions to suit this technique, and a widespread sharing of cultural values across all classes of society. By contrast today the building technique most economically employed in rural houses is fundamentally altered. Craft traditions have given way to off-site machine production, and we live in a society exposed through travel, television, and rising real incomes for most sectors of the population to a wide range of cultural experiences and choices.

THE EFFECT OF TIMBER FRAME CONSTRUCTION ON APPEARANCE

The most abrupt of these recent changes has been the introduction of timber frame construction, which brings with it constraints and opportunities affecting appearance. The external cladding of timber framed houses need be no thicker than is necessary for weathering and visual requirements. It contributes nothing to structural stability and it usually contributes little to thermal insulation.

The cladding material is unlikely to be natural stone, except in small quantities in combination with other materials. Natural stone can be used to clad timber frame, but, especially if it is laid traditionally, the walls will be thick and the costs high.

Commonly the external cladding is thin. External claddings can be chosen from a wide range of materials, including timber weatherboarding, but the most commonly used at present in Scottish rural areas are brickwork or blockwork secured across a cavity with flexible metal ties. Facing brickwork, and various types of facing block or artificial stone, are sometimes used for all or part of the cladding, but brickwork and blockwork claddings are more usually rendered. The external cladding is typically between 100 mm (4") and 150 mm (6") thick. Simulated stone claddings may be slightly thicker. Windows are normally set on the face of the timber frame to give a reveal depth of some 100 mm (4"). This is only marginally less than that in traditional walling, except in areas of high exposure where windows have customarily been set slightly further back.

In the UK the timber frames to walls are usually built as platform frames. Each storey is framed up from vertical studs with insulation within the cavities formed by the studs. Some variations to this method are offered but these have little effect on appearance. In typical stud frame construction external walls are braced with sheet material, usually plywood. On the outer face the sheathing is covered with a moisture barrier of breather paper applied prior to the cladding. A clear vertical cavity must be maintained between the outer face of the sheathing and the cladding. The cavity should be ventilated to prevent pressure build-up. Proprietary plastic perpend ventilators are usually used at eaves level and over windows, at every 1.5 m., although sometimes airbricks are used in gables. Eaves and verge ventilators to wall cavities need not be conspicuous in themselves, but their concealment is helped by projecting eaves and verges.

Timber frame houses are not easily adjusted to sloping sites by stepping the section, both because of moisture transfer and because of the need to accommodate differential settlement in the foundations. This can result in conspicuous underbuilding.

Where timber frames are combined with a masonry outer leaf the problem of differential shrinkage must be allowed for in the basic design and in the detailing. At eaves and verges a gap should be left above the masonry which can close as the timber shrinks. Sealing the gap is not required if it is protected by an overhang at the eaves or verges. This requirement suggests that the roof in timber frame construction should usually be considered as a "lid" and not complicated by masonry junctions which lead to problems of shrinkage. In particular, it is more straightforward to consider dormers as part of the roof and not to confuse them with the masonry cladding, and to avoid the difficulties inherent in combining the roof of a timber frame house with skew gables. The problem of support for skews on skew gables can be overcome, but only with difficulty. A 225 mm (9") external leaf must be provided, or the normal thickness of external leaf needs to be corbelled inwards, to support the weight of the skews, if the risk of misalignment due to differential movement is to be avoided. A thick external leaf may be desirable if a chimney is in the gable.

Pitched roofs with insulation at ceiling level should be ventilated to minimise the risk of condensation. This ventilation is normally at eaves level on opposite sides of the roof to allow cross ventilation. An eaves overhang is the most straightforward means of providing this, although other solutions including the use of a fascia board are possible.

Where external walls are rendered, it is important to prevent frost damage caused by rainwater penetrating behind the render, by providing projections around openings and at the head of the rendering to shed water away from the surface. Areas of rendered wall should normally be protected at their head by overhangs. These need not be large, but flush skews do not give adequate protection to the render where walls are rendered over blockwork or brick. BS 5262 Code of Practice: External Rendered Finishes strongly recommends overhanging eaves and verges particularly in conditions of severe exposure. BS 5642 Pt 2 recommends an overhang of 45 mm (1 ³/₄") at cills and copings. Traditional small projections of slate of some 25 mm (1") over the face of rendered walls at eaves need very careful detailing if they are combined with eaves ventilation and, as they must be in timber frame construction, with shrinkage gaps. Traditional projections of slate of 25 mm (1") over the face of rendered gables at verges would not give protection to a movement joint and have to rely on movement between the sarking and render to take care of differential settlement, and this may be insufficient.

These factors taken together suggest that skews, and traditional tight eaves and verges, are not as a general rule appropriate to timber frame houses clad in rendered masonry.

There can be exceptions to this general approach. Skews and variants of them can give useful protection to roof coverings in areas of extreme exposure to high winds. Special details for skews using a thick outer leaf of walling to provide support, and metal flashings, or coverings to upstands, to prevent water entering the cavity can be successful in these circumstances. Alternatively a raised fillet clad in metal can be used to give edge protection to roof coverings, and when combined with projecting verges appears better suited to timber frame construction. In areas of extreme exposure to high winds the risk of storm damage to overhanging eaves and verges (and of excesssive wind noise) can outweigh the risk of damage to rendering resulting from inadequate protection or inadequate allowance for differential movement. In coastal areas exposed to high winds, but where there is a reduced risk of frost, tightly fitting eaves and verges, with traditional small overhangs, if carefully detailed, can be a reasonable alternative. There can be other circumstances where the designer values the crisp geometry of tight eaves and verges for its own sake, or for contextual reasons, and providing special care is taken with detailing the practical problems can be overcome.

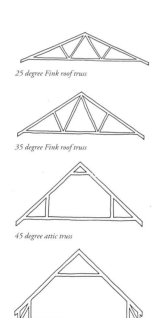

25 degree Fink roof truss

35 degree Fink roof truss

45 degree attic truss

45 degree stub attic truss

Trusses

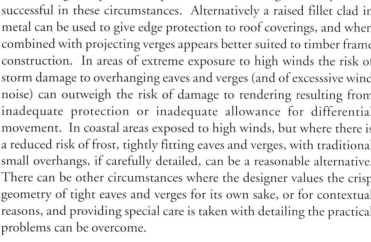

Cavity construction needs water-tight cavity trays and damp-proof courses around openings if masonry cladding is used in combination with timber frame. Complicated damp-course details around wall-head dormers, oriels and other intricate forms call for care not only in design but also in construction and supervision if they are not to fail. There is a strong practical argument for keeping wall planes and eaves lines simple.

Rybats (quoin stones) and other dressed masonry details can not be justified functionally in timber framed houses although they are often reproduced decoratively. The original nature and purpose of rybats - large dressed stones used to give strength and a true edge to rubble walls - has no equivalent when the cladding is only some 100 mm thick.

Modern harling, whether wet-dash or dry-dash, when applied to block or brick does not match the texture of traditional thin harling or lime coating, applied to uneven rubble work, although efforts can be made to make it look less uniform.

Prefabricated trussed rafters are usually the most economical method of roof construction, both for roofs without rooms and for roofs with attic rooms. Standard designs are available for both conditions. Standard designs are also available for one and three quarter storey construction (stub attic trusses) which allow the eaves line to be above the upper floor level, and consequently the upper floor width to be greater than when attic trusses of triangular section are used. Stub attic trusses are designed to avoid lateral thrust being transmitted onto the outer walls, which they are unable to resist when timber framed. Alternatively purlins spanning between cross walls can be used to provide a one and three quarters storey section, with rooms in the roof, if the plan is suitable.

Turned-down bargeboards, and simulated rybats.

The most common form of projecting eaves detail used with modern timber frame kits has a horizontal soffit, some 300 mm (1' 0") wide, at the level of the window head. With this detail, when thin masonry cladding is used, there are no lintels below the eaves and the external skin is only carried up to the level of the window head: the horizontal soffit of the projecting eaves is extended inwards to meet the head of the window at the window openings. This boxed eave, or boxed soffit, detail, apart from its intrinsic clumsiness, can produce a very awkward junction with the bargeboard if the verge is similarly projected: the bottom corners of the bargeboard have to turn down to master the width of the soffit.

This appearance of a "club foot" at the bottom corners of the bargeboard can be avoided, with thoughtful detailing. There are several options. The neatest solution is to provide lintels or false lintels, and therefore reveal a slightly greater height of wall, to expose sloping soffits, either with or without exposed rafter ends, and to keep the bargeboard plain without any downturn at its end. There is no extra cost in using this detail in a one and three quarters storey house, for which lintels must in any case be provided.

Metal sheet roofing and high performance membrane roofing materials are used extensively outside the UK for new houses and have some practical and economic advantages over the slated and tiled roofs which are almost universally used in Scotland even in new houses. Their introduction would bring profound changes to the appearance of timber frame houses, because they can be laid satisfactorily to much shallower pitches than are customary for slates and tiles.

A logical cladding material for timber framed construction is timber weatherboarding. Many of the constructional arguments for the use of timber framing apply equally to the use of timber cladding: erection is dry and less prone to delays from bad weather, and the components are easily transported. Inspection and repairs are simple. The cladding can take up small movements in the frame without cracking. There are strong environmental arguments for its use. The use of modern stains makes maintenance reasonably economical.

There is no reason why timber cladding should not be adequately durable providing it is selected and used properly, and well maintained. Timber cladding is widespread in North America and Scandinavia. Yet in Scotland the material has a bad image in the market, with customers, with planning officials and with mortgage lenders and insurance companies. It is widely associated with temporary shacks and outbuildings. The reason is probably that Scottish timber used as cladding has performed poorly in the past, and suitably durable stains have not been available until recently. Close-grained imported timber suitable for cladding is now readily available. Suitable home-grown timber is available in limited quantities and more is likely to be available in the future.

Except in climates exposed to extremes of driven rain, where maintenance costs will be higher and where there is some practical value of a rendered blockwork outer skin as a weatherbreaker, the widely-held perception that a masonry outer wall is much more durable than a well-specified timber one is probably based more on association with traditional construction than on current performance.

Some recent research and development work in Scotland and Scandinavia into timber framed houses is pointing to the desirability for the outer wall to "breathe" rather than to rely on vapour membranes to avoid interstitial condensation. Such conclusions if they become widely accepted, taken together with the need to maintain a clear cavity behind masonry cladding (which is difficult to ensure on intermittently-supervised rural sites), and with increasing insulation requirements, may lead to strong technical arguments for the more widespread adoption of timber cladding to timber framed houses as an alternative to masonry cladding.

Aluminium and UPVC claddings are now often used in countries where timber frame is popular. The profiles and colours are usually designed to resemble painted timber weatherboarding. The effect is harsher than timber weatherboarding, but it is claimed that maintenance costs are lower.

THE EFFECT OF CLIMATE ON APPEARANCE

Climate is traditionally a dominant influence on the siting and form of rural houses. Attention to it results in a better fit of new house designs to their natural environment, to their sites, and to the style of their existing neighbours. For design purposes, climate should be considered at the level of the region, the locality and the site. Differences can be experienced over a few hundred metres, where altitude, aspect and tree shelter combine to vary the degree of exposure.

Scotland as a whole experiences large seasonal temperature differences, generally a high rainfall, high wind speeds with driven rain and snow, large variations in the length of the day, and a low sun in winter.

Extreme variations in seasonal temperature cause problems of expansion and contraction in materials, and subsequent cracking. The climate in some regions is extremely wet throughout much of the year. Although on parts of the east coast rainfall is as low as 600 mm (24 inches) per year, in most of the west it is much higher. Annual rainfall in Fort William is 1800 mm (72 inches). This perpetual wetness affects the durability of materials.

Wind in association with rain is an even greater problem. The BRE's driving rain index shows the entire west of Scotland with a "severe" exposure grading of more than 7 m^2/s. The index rises to 10 or 15 over much of the Western Highlands and the Islands, with some areas with an index of 20. This driving rain will be absorbed by

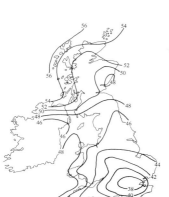

Basic wind speeds in the UK in metres/second. The map shows the maximum gust speeds likely to be exceeded on average about once in 50 years at 10m above ground in open level country.
45metres/second is the equivalent of 100mph.
56 metres/second is equivalent to 125mph.

porous materials like most brick and stone, and may also be driven by wind pressure through cracks around doors and windows, and in render, and brick or blockwork. The more water that reaches a wall the more likely it is that the material will become saturated, so that water appears at the inner face of the wall or in cavities to cause damage. At high wind speeds overhangs give little protection because the rain is driven horizontally or upwards. High wind speeds also cause structural damage, especially to tiles or slates on low pitched roofs with projecting eaves and verges. It is not unusual to experience hurricane-force winds in Skye, the Outer Hebrides and the Northern Isles. Constant wind noise is disturbing to people living in houses in highly-exposed areas. It is made worse by overhanging eaves and verges, and other projections. Houses in areas of high exposure need not only to resist being damaged by violent gales, but to look as though they do.

In designing roofs, engineers follow the guidelines of CP3 Chapter V: Part 2 1972, but it is understood this is being revised in the light of recent storm damage. General experience in Scotland indicates, as a useful rule of thumb to bear in mind when designing for high wind:

- Roofs up to 35 degrees pitch will have uplift forces on both windward and leeward slopes.

- Roofs of 20 degrees or less will have very severe uplift forces on the leeward side of the slope.

- Roofs with a pitch of more than 35 degrees are likely to have positive pressure on the windward slope (depending on topography), but negative pressure will persist on the leeward slope.

- Eaves projections call for special measures to anchor the roof to the wall head. They not only reinforce the suction forces but cause considerable wind noise.

Window pane sizes and thicknesses may be limited by wind speeds in exposed areas.

It is often believed that Scotland's climate is not well suited to solar space heating. On the contrary, the increase in the length of the heating season in the north allows a higher proportion of solar energy available throughout the year to be used in saving fuel. The likely effects on design of passive solar heating measures will be that windows on the north of the house will be small and limited in number, and there will be one or more large windows on the south side. Windows on east and west elevations should not be very large.

Houses of one and a half storeys, and one and three quarters storeys, are likely to be more energy efficient than single storey houses of the same floor area in windy climates, because of reduction in heat losses through convection in occupied rooms to the roof space, and reductions in external wall area.

Houses built for hurricanes. Traditional construction and detailing at Kyle of Lochalsh.

Architects: Hurd Rolland Partnership.

IX

DESIGN PRINCIPLES

SHARED PREFERENCES

It is doubtful whether there are any absolute principles of architectural style or composition. For example, Classicism has been claimed as a universally valid architectural language in the past (and is still so claimed by some) but it is not a style that has always enjoyed universal approval. John Ruskin and A. W. Pugin ridiculed it.

In practice, however, most designers and the critical public share loosely defined but nevertheless useful preferences about appearance which transcend the variables of context and the vagaries of taste. These are discussed in the remaining paragraphs of this section as design principles.

Architectural history confirms the evolutionary nature of style. Over long periods change occurs slowly. Only occasionally, as a result of important social or technical developments, does architectural evolution undergo a radical mutation. Out of the accumulated experience of tradition emerges a set of preferences towards architectural language and composition that can be offered as a basis for guidance. It should not be taken as a set of immutable rules, because there are no rules for design which a sensitive and imaginative designer can not break, in certain circumstances, and yet produce a successful design.

LANGUAGE

Unfamiliar architecture (including some extremes of international Modernism) is sometimes resented as a language which doesn't speak to people, or if it does so, it speaks in a language which people do not understand.

The choice of familiar language is important to acceptance. It is not enough, though, by itself. Any language should be used with purpose, to convey meaning, and be used grammatically. A modern difficulty is that present-day communications and travel have made many people familiar with languages (including architectural languages) other than those of their native land and region.

COMPOSITION AND PROPORTION

Architecture is the expression in concrete form of an idea. The same may be said of music, or painting. In these fields people speak of the *architecture* to convey the idea of a composed structure. Any idea, before it can be expressed as a composed structure in any medium, must be complete and be made up of individual elements which are related harmoniously to each other and to the unity (as distinct from the uniformity) of the overall idea. To maintain unity, it is usual for there to be a focal idea which dominates. Classical and neo-classical compositions usually stress the dominance of one element, and the idea of finiteness. Some modern compositions stress indeterminacy. Common to most systems of composition is the idea that there should be no hesitation or weakness.

Since antiquity architects have sought harmony in shape and size of the parts of buildings so that they are felt to be well ordered. Renaissance and neo-classical architects have set out to demonstrate that harmony is achieved by the unifying effect of proportion, that is to say by ensuring that the ratios in a building are simple arithmetical functions and that the ratios of all the parts of a building - its shapes, the sizes of rooms, and the dimensions of windows and doors and their relationships to facades - are either those same ratios or related to them in a direct way. A series of theorists, writing up to this century, have traced analogies between architectural proportions and the proportions of the human form and face: for example the relationship of roof to facade can equal the height of a forehead by comparison with the rest of the human head. Others have based systems of proportion on the Golden Section, a ratio of 1 : 1.62 in the sides of a rectangle.

It might be thought that these disciplines only applied to important public buildings, but the composition of Scottish houses built in the 18th and 19th centuries was governed by simple geometric ratios (squares and the repetition of certain angles) in the proportioning of their facades and the windows in them.

To what extent rational systems of this kind produce effects which the eye and mind can consciously apprehend is uncertain. The stability and power of shapes which are definite and unhesitating may be helped by simple mathematical ratios. The real point of mathematical proportioning systems may be that their users need them; that there are types of inventive mind which need such disciplines.

Consistent mathematical ratios, whether they have an anthropometric or geometric basis, between the height and length of a facade, or between the height and width of a window, are helpful tools for the designer, but they do not by themselves make a weak design much better. Far more important to design unity is the adoption of a clear and unhesitating compositional idea, and the relating of all parts of the design to it.

BALANCE AND SYMMETRY

As in nature, the quality of balance in architecture is restful. The balanced composition sometimes leads to symmetry, but symmetry is not always appropriate in a small house. The characteristic of the domestic plan is the lack of an obvious "dominant" which is the key to monumental layouts. The various rooms are too similar in their importance. The classical concept of finiteness (ie that nothing can be added to or subtracted from the composition without harming it) is associated with symmetry: in practical terms it works against flexibility and extensibility of layout.

Symmetry can be a key to the successful design of small rural houses, but more usually designers concentrate on obtaining a simple unity of form which contains all the small competing details of the domestic scene in an informal, balanced composition.

INTEREST

It is not enough for satisfactory composition that the proportions are good and that the design is unified. The composition should have interest. Good proportioning in each element provides some interest in itself, but the relationship of the elements to each other ought to be interesting also. This interest can be found through deliberate contrast, although care must be taken to avoid disunity by its unconsidered use. The Scots architect Sir Robert Matthew used to say that a feeling of excitement and lightness was given to a building if there were sharp contrasts of scale between the size of its features, an approach now in vogue among architects who use contrasting very small windows and other accents to enliven an otherwise bland facade of large elements.

INTELLIGIBILITY

When the designer's intentions are clearly revealed the building is said to be intelligible. The whole performance of the building, its convenience, durability, and appearance (its Commoditie, Firmness and Delight, the three conditions of architecture, as they were described by Sir Henry Wotton in the 17th century) are brought together as a unified whole and revealed clearly. Economy in the means of this expression is the key to this achievement.

Houses are usually simple buildings. If they are to be seen to be fit for their purpose, their appropriate expression will be terse and direct.

X

ARCHITECTURAL CONGRUITY

SCOTTISHNESS

Undoubtedly the main contributor to the Scottish vernacular has been the use of stone for walls. Another broad generalisation is that much of the vernacular which we recognise as the rural classical tradition has had clear geometric shapes: the walls have appeared to dominate the roofs, eaves have been flush, and skewed gables and dormers in the plane of the wall have anchored the the roof to the ground. These characteristics are widely associated with Scottish domestic architecture. Yet in many parts of Scotland roofs of 19th century houses overhang the masonry walls at the eaves and at the gables. This is true not only in inland parts of the Lowlands but also in the more wind-sheltered parts of the Highlands. These houses are equally a part of the vernacular. A definition of Scottishness by reference only to a particular geometry - the way walls relate to roofs - is obviously too narrow. It may be that the architects of this century - and there have been many - who have been attracted to simple sharp-edged forms and have justified this preference on historical or nationalistic grounds, have simply been expressing an understandable (given the artistic climate of their time) predilection for cubism.

How would we recognise the essential Scottishness of new houses in the countryside which are framed in timber, or built in some other new building technique, or of new houses to suit modern lifestyles? All that can be offered, with any conviction, in reply to this question is the suggestion that the answer lies, not necessarily in the traditions of unaffordable stonework and of a now-diminished agricultural economy, but in the characteristics of the land and the people: a harsh, wet and windy climate; an often wildly beautiful large-scale landscape; clear air; low light in winter; stark contrasts of snow and forest; a resilient people, direct, loyal to their communities, respectful of quality, generally reticent. If these conditions resulted in an architecture which looked sturdy and durable, clear-cut, honest about its construction and its purpose, and valuing quality rather than show, then it might claim to be Scottish.

RURAL CHARACTER

The character of buildings in the countryside, by contrast with suburbia, is rooted in practicality. Suburbia, when it invades the countryside, is recognisable by tameness and trivialisation. The large picture windows may be strong enough to withstand strong winds in practice; but if they don't look as though they do they suggest a taming of natural forces. The half-gables in artificial stonework may help to sell the house, but they suggest transient design values.

The definition of rural architectural character, and the benchmark for judging the appropriateness of new houses in the countryside, comes down, therefore, not only to the test of architectural congruity: to looking like other houses in the countryside. Nor does it come down only to simple rules about building geometry: to window proportions or roof overhangs. It comes down to respect for the power of nature, and with it an evident sense of shelter in siting, form and detail, a sense that the construction works well and is durable, and a sense of harmony with the landscape and with neighbours.

Necessarily the architecture of the past that derived from functional imperatives had a sense of homogeneity. How should new buildings relate to this?

The coherence of a group of buildings can be appreciated even if it can not be seen in a single view. A sense of harmony between the buildings and of historical continuity can sometimes be felt over a wide area. New buildings can enhance their setting by contributing to this sense.

There are two related arguments for doing so. The first rests on the idea of composition: there should be design harmony between the parts and a sense of unity of the whole. This principle can be applied to groups of buildings as validly as to a single building. Appreciation of this sense of harmony and unity holds good independently of any historical value the buildings in the group may have: it would apply equally if all the neighbouring buildings had been built recently. The second rests on the idea of conservation: it applies when the buildings in the group are valued for their historical or special architectural character. Conservation is a fine art term meaning work done to consolidate and protect the original fabric. It can be applied to places: areas, towns, villages, townships and hamlets. Its main principle is the keeping alive of places. The conservation case is that new buildings should not spoil, but enhance their historic settings: the architectural heritage should be respected and its character protected and strengthened. Old buildings give us our most immediate and tangible contact with history: respect for them preserves a continuum between past, present and future.

A new house (in this case in blockwork construction) at Waternish, Skye. It fits well with its setting even though the designer has not attempted to copy every detail of the neighbouring building.

Designer: Peter Thomas

Photo: The Scottish Office

Where vernacular traditions are intact and can be felt over a wide area, as they can over most parts of rural Scotland, these two arguments come together and reinforce each other. They lead to a policy that in these situations new buildings should complement the general character of the buildings among which they are set. This policy has public and professional support, and is recognised in legislation.

It does not follow though in all circumstances, or even in most circumstances, that new buildings need to copy all the stylistic elements or the details of the buildings in the neighbourhood. The word complement means to complete, not to copy. Examples from the past teach us that coherence depends on the general scale and grain of the group, and the typical forms, materials and colour of the locality, rather than on uniformity in the details of style. This can be seen in many of our best villages and towns, where there is a cheerful mixture of styles and types of detail. There are lessons here for the future. The best conservation policies do not confuse the evidence of history. The maxim of the British Society for the Protection of Ancient Buildings (founded in the 19th century), that old work should as far as possible be left alone and that new work should be plainly seen to be new, is as valid today as it was when it was first propounded.

There are places, such as in conservation areas, where the unity of architectural form may be important. In the great majority of cases, however, the guiding rule should simply be that new buildings should not spoil the enjoyment of existing buildings nearby or the wider environment - they should enhance it - and to do this, they need to sing in harmony, but they do not need to sing in unison.

Congruity reinforces the sense of identity of an area, which is derived from distinctive regional and local styles. R. J. Naismith identifies twelve separate character zones on the Scottish mainland (excluding the Isles) and even within these there are minor variations of character.

CONTRAST

There are many examples in Europe (though fewer in Scotland) of new buildings which interact successfully with their old neighbours, and which enhance local character, by the use of contrast - sometimes bold, sometimes subtle. New lifestyles, new forms of construction, and a developing culture will lead to developments in style. Architecture needs to experiment if it is to evolve and grow in confidence.

XI

STYLE

STYLE AND TASTE

It is a common misunderstanding that architecture is something which is "added on" to functional design, and that it is this something that creates style. The opposite is true. Style is the outcome of the whole activity of design. While style reflects the whole design process, and is relatively passive, taste is more concerned with superficial appearance, and involves greater choice, whether individual or collective.

New forms and details for a new lifestyle, interacting successfully with older neighbourhoods at Gullane, East Lothian.

Architect: Roland Wedgwood.

Frank Lloyd Wright, the American architect, used to say *'Build with style, not in a style'.* W. R. Lethaby, writing in 1920, made the same point in a different way: *'Style in a reasonable and universal sense is equivalent rather to stylish than to a style; it interpenetrates the whole texture of a work; it is clearness, effectiveness, mastery, often it is simplification.'*[18] In contrast, 'a style' is a museum name for a phase of past art. As a means of classifying what is past the style labels are useful. But once it is accepted that these styles were the outcome of circumstances which are no longer present, then it must be accepted that they can not be copied and represented as authentic outcomes of today's conditions. To design "in a style" is to design a pretence, which stands in the place of style as properly understood.

Style evolves: taste is transitory. Everyone knows what good taste is; it is his or her own taste. Someone else's taste is bad taste. One man's meat is another's poison. The cycle of taste - from modishness to disfavour, and then to camp revival - is too rapid to fit easily with objects so permanent as houses. In the mid-20th century the notion of "good" design was advanced as a means of formalizing the tastes of a liberal elite, but even these ideas are now lost in uncertainty. The volatility of taste rules out such a thing as objective good taste, and leaves only transitory preferences.

Taste is at the heart of motivation in consumption. Ideas about group membership are important in most consumer advertising and the consumption which follows from it. Suppliers of timber frame assemblies for houses, like other advertisers and manufacturers, are in competition with each other and are aware that discrimination is a stimulus to consumption. They look for unique marketing propositions, and are alive to the aspirations of their customers, including upward pressures for social mobility. One of the threats to the development of an honest modern vernacular is that the prospects for individual customers of social and material progress are often accompanied by a taste for historical retreat.

Short-term commercial competition can have consequences for design which undermine long-term quality. Car manufacturers in Detroit in the 1950s and 1960s, committed to an annual model change, abandoned improvements to the suspension, transmission and engines, but added extra chrome and fittings, styled to suit the fashions of the day, to market their products. There may be a temptation for designers of houses to do the same.

Each generation has its own rules, even if these are only culturally and socially conditioned preferences, including the expression of group tastes in architecture. Where individuals overstep the boundaries of these rules, in something so visible and permanent as a house, it is understandable if public criticism follows. In searching for the balance to be struck between public and private interests, a distinction has to be drawn between aspects of appearance which flow from shared values and are likely to change slowly, and those which are individualistic and volatile.

HONESTY

When a building is said to be "honest" in its expression the general convention is that its construction and purpose are made clear by the designer, not simply by association of ideas, but through a direct conveying of means and ends. The dignity of Scottish traditional houses arises from the directness and honesty with which their materials were used.

The themes of authenticity and meaning in architecture, though not new ideas, have been central to the modern movement since its beginnings, and especially since its development in the Arts and Crafts movement. A distinction, for the sake of clarity, has to be made here between Modernism (which is now recognised as a style, associated with a demand for an open breach with the past, and with overt technical display) and the modern movement, which is better described as an attitude than a style. The modern movement (the attitude) begat Modernism (the style), but is not limited to it. The concerns of the modern movement have been fitness for purpose, truth to materials, and responsiveness to culture. It is self-evident that as these develop, so style will develop. Modern design is progressive, respectful of the past, and builds in each generation on previous work. It is in this sense that the word modern is used in this report.

We all know what is meant by calling a brick wall more authentic than a plasterboard one covered in brick wallpaper. This can stand as a starting point for comparing the modern concern with authenticity with Post-Modernist concerns with pastiche, and a fascination for surface effects. The former deals with the nature of things: the latter with effect. The former leads to simplicity and economy in the means of expression: the latter with associations with other styles and techniques. The claim of the Post-Modernists is that through the techniques of imitation and allusion architecture raises itself above the mere contingencies of building and sets symbols for recognition. In the hands of sophisticated and literate designers, these techniques can add wit and lightness. In the hands of less good designers they lead to pretentiousness and schmalz. As Jerome K. Jerome said, *'It is always the best policy to tell the truth. Unless of course you happen to be a very good liar'.*

Both authenticity and traditional association are associated with social and moral values. Authenticity to function and construction is understood to be honest. Plainness also carries moral overtones. The notions of plain living and high thinking are embedded in Scots culture.

Yet references to traditional styles (even when not authentic) can also carry a moral message. They evoke timeless values associated with the home - strength of family, security and comfort. These values are attached to traditional design even in places where design unity is not an issue. For example, new tract housing is currently being built in the deserts of California (where there is not another house in sight) in a variety of "traditional" styles, including Elizabethan Tudor.

Timber frame can be adapted to historically derived forms and distinctive detailing, as in this house in Clydesdale.

Designers: The Border Design Centre.

New houses in the Scottish countryside will be built of materials and by techniques very different from those of their predecessors. They will be designed, however, within the context of widely appreciated, and still relatively intact, vernacular traditions. Timber frame is very versatile. It can, for example, easily be adapted to historical forms and details. But this freedom brings with it the responsibility to use the versatility sensibly. The conflicting claims of association, on the one hand, and authenticity and coherence on the other, have to be resolved.

Can there ever be a single, correct approach? The architects of the closing years of the 19th century, and the early 20th century, reacting against the battle of styles between the doctrinaire toughness of the Gothic revival, and the stuffiness of Victorian classicism, adopted a free and flexible approach which combined the best of these and other elements. The resulting architecture, and its influence on design, was enlightened, relaxed, pleasant, and popular. Is a similar period of tolerance and enlightenment too much to hope for in the closing years of this century?

XII

CURRENT BROCHURE DESIGNS

A brochure prepared by a timber frame supplier will typically illustrate a range of floor plans for houses of different sizes, and a variety of treatments of the exterior, to market his products.

A sample of brochures prepared for the Scottish market has been appraised by the authors. Their aim was to survey the general characteristics of the designs illustrated and the quality of information presented, and to assess whether the designs suited the Scottish countryside.

The appraisal was limited to a desk-top study, supplemented by a limited number of field visits. Building designs should normally be judged in relation to their location and siting, but brochure designs are necessarily drawn up without regard to their setting. The assessment of brochure designs therefore had to disregard siting factors.

Overall only a small proportion of the designs marketed by brochures are intended to be, or have been, used in rural areas: the main market for the bigger suppliers is in suburban areas. Some of the medium sized and smaller suppliers however sell their designs predominantly in the countryside, and some firms based in rural districts sell virtually their entire output to self-providers building houses on individual rural plots. Because there was no information in the brochures on whether designs were meant for rural or suburban use, it was not possible to select examples for assessment on this basis. Many of the brochures therefore showed designs which were not intended for rural use. Had it been possible for the survey to be confined to houses intended for rural areas, different conclusions might have emerged.

Although some brochure designs are built exactly as illustrated especially at the less expensive end of the range, by far the majority of brochure designs are altered by the customers. Discussions with suppliers confirmed that their brochure illustrations are intended to be no more than a starting point for a virtually bespoke design process. There are many examples in the brochures of several different external characters being offered for a particular house type. Suppliers confirmed that for any particular house type the customer was encouraged to select from this range, or to mix the design characteristics offered in the range. Some secondary elements, such as windows, could be selected more or less at will from catalogues.

A representative but random sample of 201 designs was reviewed, out of a total of 613 received, taken from 32 different brochures. The sample was therefore approximately one-third of the designs received.

A desk-top assessment does not give a clear statistical basis for judging the quality of brochure-derived designs as actually built. A field study of houses as built would have yielded different results. A useful general impression can nevertheless be gained of the quality of material being offered in brochures to potential customers.

The sizes of the houses shown in the sample brochures varied widely from 48.3 sq. m. to 492 sq. m. In bands, the sample showed 10% between 0-80 sq. m. (broadly 2-bedroom houses), 20% between 81-110 sq. m. (3-bedroom houses), 27.5% between 111-150 sq. m. (4-bedroom houses) and 42.5% over 150 sq. m. (luxury houses). The brochures were generally geared towards providing large houses, with a considerable number of luxury houses.

The costs of the timber frame and joinery packages (insofar as costs were available) ranged from £106.50 per sq. m. to £309.00 per sq. m. The average was £137.75. Not all of the brochures offered prices. The prices quoted were for the timber package alone (excluding site costs, cladding and other builders work costs, and in most cases, delivery) and the specifications (concerning eg insulation and glazing) varied between brochures to a fairly large degree.

The authors found the quality of the information in the majority of brochures was inadequate to allow an accurate assessment of what was being shown. It must therefore be insufficient for a potential customer to make a considered choice between alternatives. In most cases a reliable assessment of value for money would need more information on the design and the specification. Only one of the manufacturers' brochures showed a cross section. Few showed elevations drawn to scale. Most illustrations of appearance were perspective sketches taken from only one viewpoint, giving an indication only of general character. Many of the perspective views were inaccurately drawn in relation to the plan, giving a misleading impression of size and proportions, although a few brochures were admirably clearly drawn. Some had photographs of completed houses. Very few of the brochures gave information on the energy performance of the house described. The National Home Energy Rating scheme is not yet well established outside the public sector and independent rented sector (the NHBC introduced its Home Energy Rating Scheme in November 1992) and none of the houses appraised was rated for energy efficiency.

Houses in the countryside should have porches or draught lobbies, utility rooms and adequate workshops and storage. Space is needed for a washing-machine, tumble dryer, large freezer, wet weather clothing storage, tool storage, and some houses need fuel supply for several days. A utility room near to a protected back entrance, and an integral garage are often useful. If they are not provided at the outset, the house design should preferably allow for them to be added later without harm to the unity of design of the house. Of the sample surveyed, most had these features, but many did not. Some of the plans had dining rooms which were too small to be functional, and in rural areas it is questionable whether they are needed at all. In general the plans indicated a suburban way of living.

Few brochure illustrations gave any indication of the orientation of the plan in relation to access, sunlight and privacy, although the orientation could sometimes be inferred from the internal layout. Few brochures indicated that alternative designs had been prepared for different conditions of orientation and siting in relation to the the road. In about two thirds of the plans the living room window necessarily faced the entrance side. These plans compromised opportunities for privacy and, on sites with access from the north, prevented sunlight from reaching the living room. Field visits have confirmed that kit houses with standard brochure plans often have their living rooms facing north, this being the entrance side.

30% of the sample houses had rooms in the roof. These had roofs pitched up to 50 degrees, but most of the single storey houses had roofs pitched at less than 35 degrees.

Over the whole sample only 33% had roofs pitched between 35 degrees and 50 degrees. Only about one half of the sample of brochure designs were as visually compact as they could reasonably have been. This is important because the visual impact of a house in a relatively isolated setting can be minimised by the best choice of plan, and also of section, in relation to floor area. In only about one half of the sample was the choice of number of storeys and type of section suited to the plan depth and roof pitch to give a customary balance of roof height to wall height. In very few cases did the simplicity of form, steepness of roof pitch, limited roof overhangs and limitations of window size make the houses look sturdy and durable enough for exposure to high winds and driven rain. In only about one quarter was the plan depth well-suited to a sloping site. On sloping sites, the excavation for a new house can conflict with the surrounding landform. T-shaped and L-shaped plans are likely to be less suitable for sloping sites than relatively shallow plans. Virtually all the plans were larger than traditional farmworkers cottages. Though this is an understandable outcome of modern space requirements, the larger houses had more complex shapes than are traditional in the countryside.

A popular type of L-shaped bungalow. A part of the front gable is cut away to form a porch.

In many of the single storey L-shaped houses a part of the projecting gabled wing was cut away beneath the roof to provide a covered porch, undermining the inherent symmetry of the gable, and therefore its own sense of unity and its geometric relationship to other elements. This feature is very common among built examples of standard kit houses. It derives from the desire for a deep plan in the bedroom wing to accommodate two bedrooms and a corridor. If the roof ridge is to be kept at the same height in the living-room wing, the living room wing must be some 7m or more wide, too wide to be convenient for a single room. Either an additional room, or porch, must be accommodated in this wing. A solution lies in reducing the depth of the bedroom wing.

Brickwork was used in over one half of the sample, either over the whole exterior, or as feature panels on part of it, or as a facing to underbuilding below floor level. Although brickwork is established in the vernacular in some districts, it is an alien material in most others. Its scale, colour and regular texture can appear incongruous in relation to stone, especially when the brickwork is uniform, and pointed to emphasise its regularity. In many designs disruptive features such as wall panels of contrasting materials resulted in some disunity in the design. In many of the designs examples could be seen of masonry cladding not appearing to obey the customary

A popular type of long bungalow with a garage. The asymmetry of the accommodation under the front gable is emphasised by feature panels. The lower floor level in garage allows headroom for an attic.

rules of masonry construction: these made the designs look weak. Although thin masonry cladding serves no structural purpose, it must support its own weight, and is so closely associated in appearance with load-bearing masonry that it looks uncomfortable unless it obeys familiar load-bearing rules.

In almost all cases the area of windows was greater as a proportion of total wall area than was customary in the vernacular. In very few cases did windows generally have vertical proportions. Aside from these contextual considerations most windows

appeared to have been well considered in terms of detail. Very few eaves and verges were trimmed close to the wall-head: the overwhelming majority of the designs used boxed eaves, often with clumsy bargeboard details. In a few cases skewed gables were used with a rendered finish and flush skews. About one third of the houses had chimneys.

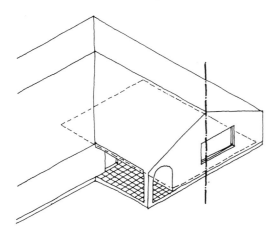

Cutting away a part of the front gable to provide a porch undermines its inherent symmetry.

Some general conclusions reached from the appraisal were that:

(a) the information contained in the brochures was in many cases insufficient to allow a potential customer to make a reliable evaluation of the designs on offer. It is recognised that, for many suppliers, the publication of brochure designs is meant to be no more than the first step in a marketing process, that further discussions with a potential client will give more detailed information, and that in any case many designs are modified, sometimes by combining elements from different designs. The fact remains that many customers select a design, or select a supplier or a builder to provide a house at a negotiated price, without going to tender, on the basis of the brochure illustrations. It is unsatisfactory that these initial decisions should be made on the basis of inadequate information about the content and performance of the house on offer.

(b) only a small proportion of the designs appraised appeared to have been specially prepared to be suitable for the countryside.

(c) a good number of designs used neo-historical external design elements entirely capriciously, without either an understanding of their original historical purpose or any benefit to the intelligibility of the design as a whole: piers clad in artifical stone which would be much too narrow to support a load if actually built in stone; artificial stone or brick veneer arches over openings actually spanned by the timber frame; fake rybats at the edges of walls built up from obviously thin slabs of artificial stone; rybats on one side of an opening but not the other. These and other offences against the grammar of construction reveal a depth of architectural illiteracy which would be surprising if it were not that we have become accustomed to it in a number of examples of house design - irrespective of construction technique - up and down the country.

A brochure design which overcomes the problem of the front gable by keeping the width of the bedroom wing and the living room wing the same.

Designer: John Peace for M & K MacLeod Ltd.

XIII

D E S I G N   G U I D A N C E

HOW TO GO THROUGH THE PROCESS

The study has shown that some customers, especially at the lower-cost end of the market and also in remote areas, choose from the designs offered in brochures almost as if they were ordering clothes by mail-order, and ask their suppliers or builders to handle all design and planning issues on their behalf. The main concerns which have been expressed to the authors about the appearance of timber frame houses in the countryside have been directed at these standard kit designs. Yet it is important that efforts to improve these designs do not price houses out of the reach of people with limited resources who need them. It is also important that simple and convenient procurement systems are available which do not deter customers who may not be familiar with dealing with professionally qualified designers.

A good standard has been reached in some recent brochure designs as a starting point for development to fit the house to its setting. When this standard of design is reached and where there are no exceptional site or planning requirements the simplest pattern-book procurement methods can be economical, convenient and effective. Although this report recommends that a much better standard of design is achieved in some other brochure examples, it does not recommend the abandonment of the use of brochure designs as a starting-point for the design process.

The recommended sequence of steps in the procurement and planning approval process is:

(1)   The planning authority prepares policies on the siting and design of new housing to bring these issues within the statutory process and to give opportunity for public comment and debate. This should allow the public, elected members, planning officials and developers to reach a consensus on the standards required.

(2)   The planning authority prepares and publishes illustrated and easily-understood design guidance for its district. The guidance may vary between character zones within the district.

(3)   Suppliers of timber frame houses commission well-qualified designers to prepare designs for houses suitable for the countryside, and make brochures available to market their products.

(4)   The intending individual client either:

(a)   selects a design from a brochure for discussion and development, and then commissions the supplier or an independent consultant to develop the design to suit his needs and the setting, or

(b)   commissions the preparation of an outline design by a supplier or independent consultant from first principles, or by significantly modifying a brochure design.

(5)   Planning permission is applied for and granted.

(6)   Detailed technical design is completed thereafter.

Whichever route is followed in the preliminary steps, design commitments should not be entered into without reasonable confidence that the planning application will receive consent. Under option 4(a) the individual client should discuss the site and design policies with planning officials before selecting the house type from a brochure. Under option 4(b), the client and designer should discuss the site and design policies with planning officials before design work proceeds.

It is important, whichever route is followed, that there is adequate design input at all three stages:

- the brochure design stage
- the client design stage, and
- the technical design stage.

Design work should always be undertaken at the client design stage, even if extra cost is involved. Consideration should always be given at this stage to siting, orientation, exterior layout and landscaping, and to the question of whether the standard brochure design needs to be modified.

THE ROLE OF THE SUPPLIERS

Not every customer is willing to employ, or can afford, an independently employed architect or skilled designer to design a timber frame house from first principles. Most customers will use brochure designs as the basis for development. They will either approach a supplier direct or engage independent professional advice from the outset to help with selection and development. Whichever method is used, it is likely that many customers will rely on the designs in brochures to help them with early design choices. The first and most direct method, therefore, by which suppliers could improve the design of timber frame houses would be by employing or commissioning the best available designers at the brochure design stage. They should take care with the selection of consultants, and visit examples of their work. Suppliers should extend and improve the ranges in their brochures so as to make the houses illustrated more suitable for use in rural areas. Not only would this improve the houses selected and built without substantial modification, but it would also provide a better starting-point for discussions on changes.

Customers would be able to make a better choice between alternative design options, and to visualise the results of their decisions, if information in brochures was factually more complete and better presented. Where customers seek out more than three or four competitive quotations, the final price can show significant cost savings. For them to be able to do this without the expense of abortive enquiries the brochures should give all the information needed to allow a preliminary comparison of what is on offer. A second means, therefore, by which suppliers could improve the value for money, including the design value, of their product would be by improving the quality of information in their brochures.

A third method by which suppliers could improve the design quality of their product as built, would be by encouraging an adequate design input at the client design stage. Brochure designs should always be developed to suit not only the client's needs but also the requirements of the setting, in terms of siting, orientation, exterior layout and landscaping, and in terms of fitting into the forms, materials and colour of the architectural setting. It would be helpful if brochures made it clear that designs are capable of being modified. Suppliers and their agents should encourage their clients to adapt their house designs sensitively to their sites, and stress that the brochure illustrations are indeed, as claimed, no more than a starting point for development. Some customers will obtain independent professional design advice at this stage, and others will contract with the supplier to provide this advice either from in-house staff or from the supplier's consultants. Whichever method is used, the house design should be developed to be appropriate to its context. Some planning authorities already recommend in their published design guidance that intending individual providers should seek professional advice from the outset so that proposed houses are better related to their sites and meet their requirements for design quality. No amount of planning control can turn a bad design into a good one: it can only make the design marginally less bad. The remedy lies in better design.

Where a design-and-build service is provided, experienced and qualified staff should be the customer's main point of contact, not a salesman or junior draftsman. Manufacturers of timber frame houses who are members of SCOTFI are aware of the need for quality assurance in construction. This same quality control is needed in design.

One difficulty is that suppliers are in commercial competition with each other, and each is looking for a marketing advantage. Their search for a unique selling proposition too often finds its outlet in product styling, achieved through additions to the basic design such as "feature panels" of contrasting materials. The approach debases the idea of quality, and can actually reduce quality in the practical and aesthetic sense. Suppliers should be encouraged, by all concerned with the public interest in amenity, to market their products on more substantial characteristics of quality: durability, convenience and economy in use; environmental standards such as energy efficiency and the use of products from sustainable resources; and architectural harmony in the design of the house itself and in relation to its setting.

THE ROLE OF THE CUSTOMERS

Customers have an interest, legitimate up to a point, in expressing their individualities through their house designs. Within the private sector, individual providers can be expected to make distinctive design choices.

Customers for timber frame houses and their designers should however be aware that society has become increasingly aware of environmental issues; that we have a precious heritage of landscape and buildings which needs to be protected; that our well being — cultural, social and economic — depends on its enhancement; that buildings are relatively permanent and unavoidable by the passer-by. Building a house in the countryside can not be regarded simply as a private transaction. There is a public interest in the result. Above all, new residents in the countryside should try to avoid importing the characteristics of suburbia.

Customers have a responsibility to others, as well as to themselves, to be discriminating in their choice of designers This applies whether they are contracting for a design-and-build service or with independent design consultants. It is important that independent designers are experienced in the limitations and opportunities of timber frame construction. When choosing architects or designers, clients should satisfy themselves that the firms they are considering have the resources for the project, including good design ability. The differences in fee charges between the different methods and firms under consideration will be small by comparison with the overall cost of the project, and can often be recouped by cost savings resulting from competition for supply and construction, and from skilful design.

Design awareness among individual providers developing houses for themselves, and a sense of public responsibility for good neighbourliness, can not easily be enforced, but it is important that it is encouraged through education, information and debate.

THE ROLE OF THE PLANNERS

Planning authorities have the task of bringing environmental objectives into a common focus with economic and social objectives.

The current reassessment of the post-war policy of restraint over development in the countryside is bedevilled by the issue of proliferation. Examples of good design show that it is possible for houses to be located and designed so as not to spoil the landscape. But if they accept one house in the landscape, how do planners refuse another, and then another? One approach is suggested by West Lothian's farm restructuring policy. *'We now have pressure to revitalise less favoured areas, pressure to meet local needs in sought-after areas, and a substantial suppressed demand from people who would like to establish a rural lifestyle or business. A remarkable opportunity now presents itself to end the period of fossilisation which has prevailed since the war and to allow the rural settlement pattern to continue to evolve once more in ways which meet both individual and wider public interests...For the first time farmers now have a positive interest in joining with planners to look at the management and development of the whole farm. And it is this whole farm approach which offers a solution to the precedent issue. There is a powerful tool known as a Planning Agreement (a Section 50 Agreement in Scotland). It can regulate the use of a whole land unit such as a farm, regardless of future changes of ownership, to make an otherwise unacceptable development approvable...In some places the rewards may not outweigh the possible risks. In others they may be very considerable - our ordinary countryside could be transformed very much for the better'.*[19] A recent architectural competition for detached houses and workshops in three locations in West Lothian, has shown what can be done.

This report has drawn attention to the threat to rural architectural character which comes from suburbanisation. It is arguable that new residents who come to the countryside and who do not wish to fit in with its traditions and values spoil the rural

Where there is an obvious functional connection between the house and agriculture or work-place, even the simplest small bungalow looks at home. This standard kit house fits comfortably into its crofting setting in Lochaber.

Designers: Campbell Homes.

environment not only for their rural neighbours and for visitors, but also for themselves. Would it be preferable for them to meet their housing needs in fewer, and relatively large, new settlements than in a proliferation of additions to existing communities which swamp the character of the villages and townships to which they are attached?

Planning authorities are unlikely to achieve all their aims by compulsion. They will need to spread awareness of a vision of an improved countryside, offering realistic opportunities, allowing scope for self-determination, and following through with guidance and support.

The right approach to development control will vary according to the location. The impact of proposed houses on their landscape setting and on the architectural character of the area will vary according to (a) their prominence, and (b) the sensitivity, unity and quality of the setting. Most sites in the countryside are prominent, but not all are. Design unity and congruity with vernacular traditions can be important locally, but there are places where the bulk of development is recent and where congruity with neighbouring development would be an unnecessary aim. The overall strategy for design improvement should be strong: its application in detail will need to be flexible as between one area (or site) and another.

Design policies and development control decisions should be based on agreed criteria, drawn up in a climate of a well-informed and lively awareness of design principles and local character. It would be unreasonable to base planning decisions on the imposition of personal taste.

For the mainstream of new houses across the countryside, good quality, modern, design should be the norm and not the exception. An understanding of, and respect for, the local vernacular, and respect for the scale and character of traditional housing in the area, provides a sound basis for agreed policies, but planning authorities should not expect the application of a list of vernacular details to achieve the necessary quality. What is needed is that the houses should be well sited and good neighbourly. In most cases it will be sufficient that they should look fit for their purpose, honest, sound, human and pleasant. They should draw on traditions of Scottish house design in a general sense of directness and orderliness, and, wherever congruity is important, on local traditions of overall shape, scale, materials, and character. But, other than in a few special cases, they should not be asked to copy the past in a detailed sense. Providing the requirements of good-neighbourliness are met, quality is what matters.

In their development control role, planning authorities ought to keep in mind the difference between genuine coherence with the local vernacular and vaguely neo-historical taste.

Most planning authorities would agree that it would be wrong to prohibit personal expressions of taste in transient detail, such as carriage lamps or garden ornaments, unless they interfered with broader design policies. What about semi-permanent but reversible features such as neo-historical window and door details (Elizabethan leaded window lights and Tudor doors) and other permanent building details such as simulated window margins and quoins - whose introduction may owe more to taste than to any genuine need for congruity with the local vernacular? This is difficult territory and each case needs to be judged on its merits. A reasonable starting-point would be to avoid making blanket rules which either require or prohibit these features. Broader design policy objectives for the building in its setting, and the integrity of each building design, should be the basis for decisions.

Planning authorities, working within the statutory process of public comment and debate, have to bear in mind the interests and rights of the individual. For some individuals the extra costs of meeting planning requirements can price the house out of reach, and for this reason it is important that there are no unnecessary restrictions. For many the design and construction of a house is an act of self-expression, and may be intended as a deliberate break with the past; and room should be left in planning guidance and the planning control process for imagination and the development of style.

WHERE TO BUILD

The character of the Scottish landscape varies widely. In parts it is untamed. In parts it has been subdued by cultivation. Different landscapes reflect geological and climatic conditions. In the past these have influenced settlement patterns and building methods. [20]

Change in the landscape is slow. The public perception is that the rate of change in the countryside brought about by new development should be organic, and that new buildings should adapt themselves to the visual scene. Lessons can be learnt from looking at the ways in which traditional buildings have been set in the landscape. Rural builders have sited houses in particular positions with good reasons: wind shelter, sun, slope, spacing, and visual harmony

New houses of modest importance should not dominate the landscape but integrate themselves with it. The impact can be reduced by using existing or newly-planted trees next to the building group or as a backdrop, by avoiding skylines and elevated positions, and by the choice of building form. Sites with natural features of slope and vegetation are usually more satisfactory than those which are flat or featureless.

Where grouped patterns are traditional, the creation of new clusters, reflecting the grouping of farm buildings, is likely to suit the landscape better than isolated sporadic development. A cluster of new houses near Elgin, in Moray.

Photo: The Scottish Office

The existing pattern of development in an area should be respected. In some districts, for example, there are two different patterns of development: a dispersed pattern and a grouped pattern. In such an area there might be a site within a small group suitable for infill, or a new development might relate well to an existing house or steading to form a cluster. In most cases the impact is minimized if new buildings are associated with existing settlements. One cottage in an isolated setting may not intrude unpleasantly: it may emphasise the remote character of the landscape, providing clues to its scale, and giving an assurance of shelter. But as a general rule, where attachment to existing settlements is not practicable, and where grouped patterns are traditional, the creation of new clusters, reflecting the grouping of farm buildings and acting as wind breaks, is likely to suit the landscape better than isolated sporadic development. Ideally land assembly should be organised to allow this.

Planning authorities should include in their guidance to intending developers general advice on the location and siting of new houses in relation to the visual scene.

SCALE AND OVERALL FORM

The scale of a new house should be adjusted to its setting. A distinction can be made between large-scale and small-scale landscapes. The scale of the landscape is influenced by the length of views within it and the frequency with which it changes character. The scale of the development is determined by its bulk and articulation. Sweeping lines of landscape, rugged hills, uniform vegetation, sea and inland lochs, call for larger sized buildings or building elements, and simpler shapes. Smaller irregular valleys and undulations, smaller field patterns, varied vegetation, hedges, dykes and existing buildings, provide short range viewpoints and call for smaller scaled buildings, broken down if necessary in form or by colour to give complexity to the outline. Cowsheds and other farm outhouses had this result in the past: garages, toolsheds and boathouses can be used by the designer to do the same thing now. In some cases the appropriate scale will be determined by nearby buildings.

A new building can not only give scale, it can alter the previously perceived scale of a landscape by providing a reference point against which the landscape is judged. In

Cottage in an isolated setting in Angus. Its presence emphasises the remote character of the landscape, provides clues to its scale, and gives an assurace of shelter.

landscapes such as those in Caithness, Sutherland and the Outer Isles the scale is vast in the horizontal dimension, and is sensitive to interventions in the vertical scale. In these areas, where the landform offers little shelter, buildings have traditionally been built close to the ground and grouped to offer protection.

The impact of a house on its setting can also be affected by the choice of overall shape. This will be determined by the footprint area of the plan and by the section. A rectangular plan is usually best for a small house. In a larger house the length of the frontage can be kept within reasonable limits if there are extensions of the plan to the rear of the main frontage. For a house of moderate size a one and a half storey section or a one and three quarters storey section presents a smaller overall elevational area than a single storey house or two storey house of the same depth, and this will minimize its visual impact. But it may look awkwardly vertical if the house is small. In the case of a very small house a rectangular bungalow is usually the best solution, practically and visually. A long and unbroken large single storey house (such as the very common ranch-house type) can be very obtrusive. A steeply pitched roof over a very deep plan can also be obtrusive.

Living room windows can be at the side of the house to receive sun and improve privacy.

Planning authorities should include in their guidance to intending developers general advice on the scale and overall form of proposed designs, so that they are adapted to their landscape settings.

Individual providers should seek the advice of planning authorities on scale and form. Whether they intend to select designs from brochures or whether they intend to adapt designs, they should take account of the impact of their proposals on the landscape setting.

SITING

Many sites now being developed have slopes, and their preparation sometimes conflicts with the surrounding landform. Modern methods of excavation make it easy to terrace a flat building platform out of a sloping site. This crude approach is often taken because the house is designed for a flat site. The distortion of the surrounding contours is disruptive, especially if several adjacent houses are developed in this way, and the steep embankments or retaining walls on the downhill side of the excavation can be ugly in detail.

To reach as wide a market as possible, brochure-designed houses are usually illustrated on a flat site. Deep plans, T-shaped plans and L-shaped plans are likely to be less suitable for sloping sites than relatively shallow rectangular plans. A rectangular plan aligned parallel to the contours is usually the best option for a sloping site. Alternatively, house plans can, with care, be adapted to moderately or steeply sloping sites by the use of stepped levels and multiple levels, so as to avoid the need either for platform excavation or for excessive and ugly underbuilding.

Suppliers should prepare designs which are suitable for sloping sites, or which can easily be adapted to them, and show these design types in their brochures. When designing for sloping sites, customers and their designers should avoid large platform excavations, and either choose relatively shallow rectangular plans or adapt their plans to the slope. Underbuilding should be kept as inconspicuous as possible, and areas of blank, featureless, walling and awkward junctions between adjacent underbuilding walls, should be avoided. Excavations for roads, and the effect of likely future extensions on the setting should be kept in mind at design stage.

Few brochure designs at present on offer give a clear indication of the orientation of the plan in relation to access, sunlight and privacy, although this can sometimes be inferred from the layout. In most brochure plans the main living room windows, which should preferably receive sunlight, are shown on the same side of the plan as the entrance. There will often be a need for living room windows to be on the opposite side of the plan to the entrance or at one side of the house if they are to receive sun. This arrangement gives advantages of privacy. Where large windows are on the entrance side and the house is near to a public road, privacy will be improved if they are screened by planting.

Suppliers should make clear the intended siting of their plans in relation to access and the road position, sunlight and privacy, in their brochures, and provide alternatives for different sets of conditions.

Setting a house back from the points from which it is most likely to be viewed (usually the road) can diminish its visual impact. The visibility of the access drive needs consideration: it affects the impact of the house on its setting.

THE IMMEDIATE LANDCAPE SETTING

Planting around houses can have several purposes, but the main reason in Scotland is wind shelter. It can also be useful as a screen. Tree and shrub planting can integrate the building into the landscape. The immediate landscape setting can be used as extensions of the indoor living area, reducing the need for extensions and walls, which may be visually intrusive, to give shelter. On some extremely exposed sites, as in the Western and Northern Isles, planting for these purposes may be impracticable.

Although tarmac and concrete drives, and concrete kerbing, are sometimes a practical requirement to meet the needs of prams, wheelchairs and cars, less formal solutions usually look better in rural areas. Boundary walls, fences and hedging also need to be designed to fit with local traditions.

Individual providers and their designers should consider new planting and existing planting, driveways, boundary walls, fences and hedging at an early stage in the design process, and discuss these with the planning authority.

THE ARCHITECTURAL SETTING

The character of local vernacular housebuilding varies across Scotland. It is generally based on the dominant influence of load-bearing stone masonry construction. In settlements, and sometimes over a wide area, this often results in consistency in scale, shape, proportions, materials, and colour. It hardly ever results in uniformity. The sense of coherence of these areas arises from local conditions, from functional imperatives and from the directness and honesty with which materials were used.

If new houses are to be equally fit for present-day purposes and equally direct and honest in their use of new materials, they will look different to their neighbours. Differences in culture, new lifestyles and new forms of construction lead naturally to developments in house design. These differences may go beyond points of detail. Houses are likely to be bigger than traditional farm-workers cottages, and it will be a mistake to expect them to have similar forms. New methods of construction open up opportunities for economy, freer space planning, and larger openings, and make the copying of some traditional features impractical or inappropriate.

There are many examples of new buildings which interact successfully with their older neighbours without attempting to copy past styles. Even within a group, design unity does not require uniformity. New houses should not normally be expected to look as like old houses as possible, but care should be taken in their design that they do not spoil, but enhance, the passer-by's enjoyment of neighbouring buildings and the wider environment.

Planning authorities are recommended to include in their guidance to intending developers advice on local vernacular traditions in their areas, concentrating on the main themes which contribute to local identity, and recognising variations in character. Where there is a valuable, consistent and evident vernacular over an area, good-neighbourliness will usually require that new houses should reflect the overall proportions and shapes used locally, and where practicable the typical materials and colours also. Where the group value of a settlement is paramount, design coherence can be sustained by relating new work to the scale and grain of the group. In conservation areas there will normally be a requirement to conserve and enhance the quality of the historic and architectural environment. In these cases the materials and techniques should be as authentic as possible. If the materials and the way they are used are not authentic they degrade not only the integrity of the new work but also our understanding of the tradition they seek to emulate.

In all other situations, the introduction of detailed references to tradition should should be left to the discretion of the designer.

So as to give their customers choices which are likely to fit with the vernacular outlines of the houses in areas where they are going to build, suppliers should develop ranges of designs which reflect the overall forms of traditional rural houses. Individual providers and their designers, when selecting or adapting these designs or when designing from scratch, should discuss with the planning authority its guidance on traditions in the locality and the immediate setting, before committing themselves.

There will be circumstances where innovative design is appropriate. Not all sites are conspicuous. Not all areas have a character to which new houses should defer. Skilled designers need to be given the chance to show their abilities when freed from the contextual constraints.

In all circumstances there should be two aims: of complementing the setting, as may be appropriate; and of designing a house in which itself all the elements of design are fully resolved.

RURAL ACCOMMODATION NEEDS

New houses built by individual developers providing houses for themselves in the countryside are usually larger than the traditional farmworkers' cottages of the vernacular. The accommodation provided has not only to meet current space planning expectations but also to fit with the practical needs of rural living. Rural houses typically need porches or draught lobbies, internal space for wet and dirty clothing, plenty of storage for tools and materials, utility rooms and workshops, garages, fuel storage, l.p.g. tanks and wood stacks. As a general rule it is practical and visually desirable for these to be integral with the house, or screened. Where they are separate structures the unity of the building group should be sustained in style and scale.

Suppliers should illustrate in their brochures house plans with accommodation suitable for rural living, including plans to which ancillary rooms and garages can easily be added without harm to the design of the house.

Individual providers and their designers when adapting designs from brochures or preparing an outline design for a house in the countryside, should make sure that the accommodation is suitable and easily added to without harming the appearance of the house in its setting.

DESIGNING FOR CLIMATE

Some rural areas of Scotland are exposed to driven rain and very high winds, which can result in water penetration and structural damage to roofs, eaves and verges, and certain types of windows. The high winds, incidentally, call for care in the siting of balanced flue outlets.

Suppliers should illustrate in their brochures ranges of house designs suitable for areas of exposure to high winds and driven rain. Designers of houses in these areas should bear in mind the need for houses not only to resist exposure to extreme weather, but to look as though they do.

Not all houses will be built in areas of exposure to high wind speeds. In many inland areas, wherever a wet climate is combined with reasonable wind shelter, the 19th century tradition was for overhanging eaves and verges. The continuation of this practice in sheltered areas would be both traditional and functional.

Scotland's climate is well suited to passive solar space heating. Likely developments in this field will lead to windows being varied in size in relation to orientation, with large windows on the south. Energy can also be saved by using higher levels of insulation than are common at present and by designing with compact plans and sections. Suppliers should illustrate in their brochures energy efficient house designs related to orientation. Planning authorities should be aware of the likely effects of energy measures on design and allow for them in their policies.

FORM, COMPOSITION AND PROPORTION

There is a sturdy and orderly feel to much of Scotland's domestic architecture which derives largely from unity of form, good composition and proportion, and compactness. Designers should aim for these qualities, and avoid hesitation and weakness in composition.

To minimise the impact of a house on its setting the length of frontage of a larger house may be best kept within reasonable limits if combined with extensions of the plan to the rear of the main frontage. In this case the side elevation (which may be important because houses in the open countryside are usually seen from more

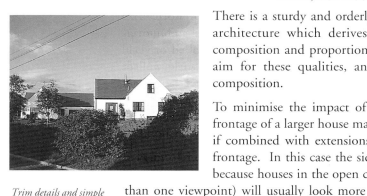

Trim details and simple forms in a pair of modified timber system houses at Blyth Bridge, Tweeddale.

Designer: Tony Winkle.

than one viewpoint) will usually look more satisfactory if the rear extension results in a T-shape, rather than an L-shape or U-shape. A rectangular plan is usually the best shape for a small house.

Pair of purpose-designed timber frame houses at Sinclairshill, Berwickshire. Unassuming and well sited against mature trees.

Designer: Frank Entwistle.

The use of consistent mathematical ratios between the height and length of a facade or gable, or between the height and width of windows, are helpful tools for the designer, but they do not by themselves make a weak design much better. Far more important to design unity is the adoption of a clear compositional idea, and the relating of all parts of the design to it.

The quality of balance in architecture is restful. A balanced composition sometimes leads to symmetry, but symmetry has associations with formality that may be inappropriate in a modern small house

Trim details in a modified timber system house at Ormiston Hall, East Lothian, with mature planting.

Designer: John C. Allan.

The composition should have interest, and this can be found through deliberate contrast in the elements, but care must be taken to avoid disunity. The use of too many materials on one elevation, and of feature panels of contrasting materials leads to disunity. Designers should avoid features which are disruptive to the unity of wall elements and to the overall composition. As a very general guide, no more than two materials should be used on an elevation above the base course (no more than one on a gable), and preferably only one.

The balance between roof height and wall height is set by the choice of section in relation to plan depth and roof pitch. Roofs in Scotland have been traditionally pitched at between 39 and 44 degrees, although there are many examples between 35 and 50 degrees, with shallower pitches predominating in the south and steeper pitches in the north. In single storey houses the height of roof is customarily between one, and one and a quarter, times the height of the wall. Because today's plans are deeper, an acceptable balance for single storey houses would be achieved if the height of roof was between one and one and a half times the height of the wall in roofs with gables. A roof pitch of 35 degrees and a depth of 7.2 m. would result in a ratio of 1:1.3 (assuming a wall height of 2.2 m.).

The problem of top heaviness when a gabled attic type roof is used with a deep plan can be overcome by using a one and three quarters storey section. This pair of houses at Woll, in Ettrick and Lauderdale, combines this type of section with entrance porches.

This combination of roof pitch, plan depth and wall height does not allow rooms in the roof. Either the roof pitch or plan depth can be increased to give the necessary space, but to provide rooms in the roof using either of these alternatives results in a ratio of substantially more than 1:1.5 and can appear clumsily top heavy in roofs with gables. This can be seen from many current designs for one and a half storey houses where the plan is deep. A ratio of more than 1:1.5 was sometimes used to give a sheltering effect in piended roofs of the late Victorian and Edwardian eras, usually with swept and overhanging eaves, and can look satisfactory. The appearance of top heaviness arises more usually with one and a half storey gabled roofs, and for these a ratio of not much more than 1:1.5 may be a visually comfortable maximum. This problem can be solved in attic type gabled roofs by using a one and three quarters storey section, thereby increasing the wall height, and revealing the lintels below the eaves line. In this option more usable area as a proportion of the plan area is obtained on the upper floor.

Wherever architectural congruity should be taken into account (as it usually should) designers should regard a pitch of 35 degrees in Lowland areas as a minimum for single storey houses. 40 degrees will usually be better. This pitch may need to be steeper in the Highlands to reflect local traditions and to give better weather resistance. Where attics are used, designers should consider either raising the eaves line immediately above lintel level in one and a half storey houses, or using a one and three quarter storey section, to improve the proportion of roof to wall. Sheeted and membrane roofs with flatter pitches need not be ruled out in some settings.

In most areas roof shapes traditionally had two equal slopes and gable ends. Piended roofs have been used to good effect in some areas for larger houses. Half-piended roofs have rarely been used. Double pitched roofs with unequal slopes have rarely been used, although monopitch extensions to cottages, usually at a different slope to the main roof, are common. Combinations of gables and piends on the same building usually look weak and unsatisfactory. So do combinations of flat roofs and pitched roofs. Piended roofs with short ridges in proportion to the length of the piends appear unresolved: they are usually less suited to small buildings. The roofs of wings or additions to buildings should not dominate the main roofs: the subsidiary eaves levels should not be higher than those of the main roof, and the major roof should predominate. Lesser roofs customarily indicate minor rooms.

Designers should aim for clarity and balance in selecting and combining roof shapes.

DORMERS

Dormers rising out of the roof plane and wall-head dormers breaching the eaves line are important in the Scottish tradition. Dormers are customarily small. False dormers (above the window head and eaves level) are not strongly represented in the vernacular, and emasculated versions of this type (small triangular gables above the eaves line, commonly called "gablets" or "eyebrows") have no part in the tradition. Large dormers, especially box dormers, spoil the roof line, upset the balance between roof and wall, and appear structurally weak. Where dormers are used, designers should aim to keep them small, and to have regard to local traditions when combining dormers with roof shapes and eaves lines.

Purpose designed timber system houses planned to reflect the forms of their Victorian canal-side neighbours, at Cairnbaan, Argyll. These houses have now become a standard brochure design type.

Designer: John Peace for M&K Macleod Ltd.

WALLS, WINDOWS AND DOORS

Although thin masonry cladding serves no structural purpose when combined with timber frame, it must support its own weight, and is so closely associated with load-bearing masonry that it looks uncomfortable unless it obeys familiar loadbearing rules. Where walls are clad in rendered blockwork or brickwork, openings should not appear so near to the corners of walls on plan, or so near to the edges of gables, that the walls would crack if they were loadbearing. Piers should look as if they are robust enough to support the loads above them, which should appear to be transferred to the ground. If simulated masonry details such as rybats and arches are used they should be used in accordance with traditional structural practice, random rubble should not appear to span unsupported over garage doors, and adequate bearing should be given to beams and lintels. In the hands of confident designers some of these guidelines can safely be set aside (for example to reveal the true nature of the timber frame, windows might be designed to wrap around the corners of walls under the eaves) but only if skill and care are used.

This approach provides an easily recognised architectural analogy with traditional construction. For example, because most windows in the classical masonry tradition have their widths limited by the span of a stone lintel, usually some 850 mm., a requirement to reflect the character of a local masonry vernacular will result in windows being vertically proportioned in all but the smallest sizes.

It would be too restrictive though to set out as a blanket requirement that window openings in masonry walls should always be vertical. Modern preferences for daylight and lower cills suggest a larger overall window area than was customary in the past. The provision of daylight in relation to room sizes and uses, requirements for sunlight, passive solar heating measures,

Purpose-designed timber frame house at Ebost, Skye.

Architect: Alasdair Alldridge of Wittets Ltd.

and the desire for good views out of the house, and direct access from living rooms to the garden, may all call for some windows to be relatively large. The practical requirement to limit spans to the span of a stone lintel is of course absent in new houses when timber frame is used: the structural support over the opening is provided by the frame, and even if masonry cladding is carried over the opening greater spans are easily achieved using steel or concrete. The requirement for visual consistency with masonry buildings nearby is not always important. Furthermore, the mixing of constructional metaphors can make the resulting expression - an essentially horizontal overall form, with projecting eaves and verges, combined with vertical openings in a masonry wall - look half-hearted in a small house. Some well-meant efforts to combine the form of a small modern bungalow with regular vertically proportioned openings have produced elevations which are very dull.

There are successful historical precedents for wider windows with horizontal proportions. The architects of the Arts and Crafts movement, such as Lorimer and Mackintosh, reacting against the limitations of classical precedents, used horizontal windows to good effect, often in broad bands immediately under the eaves, and thereby provided the basis for a popular stylistic tradition. In their time horizontal ranges of windows were usually mullioned. The mullions - evenly spaced at tradional window width intervals - gave an important vertical sub-rhythm balancing the general horizontal emphasis. Non-structural timber mullions can be used in modern horizontally proportioned windows in the same way to give the same effect, and may be appropriate for the same reasons.

The house at Gesto is
purpose-designed in
timber frame.

Architect:
Alasdair Alldridge
of Wittets, Ltd.

It is unwise therefore to lay down firm rules. The following guidelines may be useful in the majority of cases:

(a)   Where congruity with a vernacular masonry tradition is particularly important, window areas will need to be kept fairly small on public elevations. As a rule of thumb, designers should aim in these circumstances for the area of window and door openings to be not more than one third of the total wall area above floor level on publicly visible

elevations. Window spans may need to be kept to a width not much greater than the traditional width of some 850 mm, and therefore to be vertically proportioned in the case of all but the smallest sizes. Where large windows, such as patio windows leading to gardens, are required, privacy and local character can often (depending on orientation) be respected by positioning them to the side or rear of the house, or by screening.

(b) From the point of view of the overall form of the house this approach is unlikely to cause difficulties if the walls are prominent in relation to the roof, or if the house is fairly large, but care needs to be taken in a small house with a horizontal shape and oversailing eaves and verges that the effect is not mean and boring. In these cases a variety of window shapes to suit the proportions of the house may be more appropriate.

Purpose-designed house at Fanks on Skye. The timber frame has been designed in the traditional way, and assembled by a local joiner. Some elements of the house are self-built by the owners.

Architects: C. Dear and N. Thomson.

(c) There are precedents in some districts for margins, which may be painted, around windows. Their origin lies in loadbearing rubble masonry, whether harled or not, and there is no practical justification for them in timber frame construction. Their use may be justified in some circumstances to match the local architectural context, or for their associational or decorative value: to provide a point of emphasis or to soften the junction between wall and window. There should not be a blanket requirement for them to be used.

The interior of the house at Fanks. The living room is opened up through two storeys, adding cross views and varied daylighting to the experience of interior space.

Photo: Nick Thomson

(d) In areas where local consistency is not an important issue, and in the hands of skilled and literate designers, these general guidelines can be broken successfully, and clues to the true nature of the timber frame - such as a greater freedom on window design - can be laid to develop style. These freedoms should be used with care. It takes a good designer firstly to understand the traditions and then to know how to bend the rules.

Timber frame walls need to rest on a masonry base. Where walls are rendered, the base is often revealed faced in another material, such as brickwork. The base can look obtrusive and the building itself can sit awkwardly above the landscape. Efforts should be made to reduce this effect by keeping the visually differentiated base to the minimum, or by the choice of colour, without compromising sound building practice.

Heavy-handed efforts to make masonry walls cladding a timber frame look as though they are carrying loadings greater than the size of the house suggests, such as the use of arches and heavily rusticated artificial stone, should be avoided.

Many of the design difficulties which arise when timber frame is combined with masonry cladding are resolved when the cladding material itself is timber or another non-loadbearing material.. The current perception that timber cladding is less durable than an outer wall of masonry is probably based more on association with traditional construction than current practice. Except in climates exposed to extremes of driven rain which might result in high maintenance costs, every encouragement should be given to individual providers and their designers to use the design opportunities offered by timber cladding.

Purpose-designed timber frame extention to an old schoolhouse at Feshiebridge, in Badenoch and Strathspey. The walls are clad in untreated cedar and the roof in cedar shingles.

Architect: David Skinner.

Award winning purpose designed timber frame house at Weem, in Perth and Kinross. The house is one of Scotland's first "ecological buildings" using non-toxic building materials and finishes, and materials from renewable resources.
The construction incorporates a timber "breathing wall" allowing the natural transfusion of air circulation. The building sits in context with its setting, the roof pitches reflecting the forms of the nearby Weem Kirk.

Architects: Howard Liddell and John Brennan of Gaia Architects Scotland.

At a detailed level of window design, thought needs to be given to the sizes of panes and their character. There is no basis in the Scottish vernacular for currently popular swept-head and Tudor-head casements. Some modern window types in which top-hung fanlights and fixed lights of varying size compete with each other for attention (though not now so common as they were) are best avoided because of their restless and disunifying effect on the elevations. Glazing panes are best kept simple and large enough for double glazing to be economical (some 420 mm square is a reasonable minimum) and their arrangement should be orderly. False astragals and false leaded lights glued to one or other of the sides of a double-glazed unit are fairly easily seen to be fakes.

COLOUR AND EXTERNAL FINISHES

Earthy colours in roofs and brickwork or blockwork, or as admixtures to or colour coatings to harling, blend with the landscape and make houses look less conspicuous, but their use for this purpose can be overdone. They can look utterly drab. There is little to recommend what Charles McKean (Secretary to the RIAS) has christened the "cowpat school of colour design": the recent epidemic of brown roofs and brown walls.

Generally it is better if roofs contrast with walls by being brighter (as when red clay pantiles are used) or darker (as when slates or slate imitations are used). Over most areas of Scotland where there is a slate roof tradition a clear definition of roof shapes, a sense of stability, and conformity with the vernacular, will be best achieved by keeping roofs dark grey.

Where walls are harled, wet dash is less uniform and harsh than dry dash and pea-harling. Lime harling is less liable to crack and appears more luminous than cement harling. Local traditions give useful clues to appropriate colours for harling: dark red, ochre, raw sienna, and cream are common as well, of course, as white and off-white. Highly uniform brickwork look can look harsh and out of character in stone-built districts.

Modern breather paints on timber cladding give scope for the use of fresh colours.

DETAILING

Traditional tight eaves and verges, and skews, are not technically well-suited to timber frame houses clad in rendered masonry, although there can be exceptions to this generality in coastal areas where high wind speeds are more of a problem than frost damage. The practical requirement to deal with differential movement suggests that, in areas of moderate exposure, the roof in timber frame construction should overhang walls, even if only by a small projection, and not be complicated by masonry junctions. There can be other circumstances where the geometry of tight eaves and verges can be valued for its own sake or for contextual reasons. If careful precautions are taken failures can be avoided. For similar reasons it is more straightforward to consider dormers as part of the roof and not to confuse them with the masonry cladding, and to avoid the difficulties inherent in combining timber frame with skew gables.

Boxed eaves are usually clumsy, especially when combined with overbearing fascia boards and heavy barge boards with "club foots". This clumsiness can be avoided by careful and neat detailing

In general a new vocabulary of details suited to timber frame construction needs to gain acceptance. The most practical direction for this new vernacular to take in the design of roof details is that of:

(a) simplicity, by the avoidance of unnecessarily complicated junctions and their associated flashings, and of

(b) greater protection, normally by the use of projecting eaves and verges on all elevations.

The use of rybats, margins and other traditional stonework details can not be justified functionally in the walls of timber framed houses although they are often reproduced decoratively. In these, as in all external details, designers should aim to reconcile an appropriate relationship to local character with authenticity to modern construction.

One common theme can be said to run throughout all the design guidance in this study, but which applies particularly strongly to the refinement of detail. It is *keep it simple*.

XIV

IMPLEMENTATION

This publication is concerned primarily with design. It is obvious, though, that the appearance of new houses in rural areas will be determined by a wider range of factors than design guidance can by itself provide.

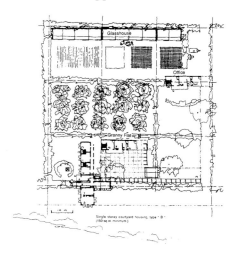

Single storey courtyard housing, type ' B '
(150 sq.m. minimum)

We are in a period of radical change. Changes in household formation, in-migrating settlement into rural areas, second-home and holiday-home pressures, and easy commuting by car, are creating a rising demand for houses in the countryside. New residents in the countryside are no longer predominantly the people who work there. Some of the practical reasons for control of rural development in the past have evaporated: the protection of food production is no longer seen as a national imperative, and farms are now looking for new uses for unproductive land. These changes, and others, are bringing about a reassessment of rural planning policy. How is the notion of the countryside to be protected? How is damaging proliferation to be avoided? The building techniques employed in the past are fundamentally altered. Craft traditions have given way to off-site prefabrication, and we live in a society exposed to a wide range of cultural choices. How are new houses to be designed so that they satisfy their owners, are economical, are evidently sensible and enjoyable in their own terms, and at the same time do not spoil the pleasure felt by others of the buildings in the immediate neighbourhood, and of the wider architectural and natural environment?

As a first step, more research is urgently needed into these issues, so that we understand them better. In particular more research is needed into the scale and spatial distribution of individual provision in the countryside, the needs of rural living, and the delivery of design services to a generally fragmented rural market. Sponsorship of this research might lie with the Government, possibly acting through Scottish Homes, the national housing agency, or with the planning authorities. The timber frame industry should be encouraged to promote research into market

Layout plan for the entry of one of the joint prize-winners in a recent ideas competition for test locations with outline planning consent under West Lothian's farm restructuring policy. This layout shows a house, a granny flat and a garage grouped around a courtyard, a small office building, and glasshouses, set out in a structured landscape defined by hedgerows and 'ha-has' to create enclosed productive gardens and moderated microclimates.

*Architect:
William Fraser Watt*

Royal Incorporation of Architects in Scotland

Sketch of one of the house types in the joint prize-winner's competition entry. The proposed walls are timber framed, rendered externally. Roofs are built of stressed skin plywood panels covered with profiled mineral fibre sheeting.

*Architect:
William Fraser Watt*

Royal Incorporation of Architects in Scotland

attitudes. More research is needed to establish the extent to which the present supply is satisfying customers, and to what extent better and wider choices are needed by rural customers. Some research needs to be targeted at the use of timber cladding, followed by development work to demonstrate design opportunities which would be opened up by its greater use.

Policy development is the logical second step. In practice the development of planning policy by Government and planning authorities is an evolutionary and iterative process, and policy continues to be developed. Some planning authorities have recently published new and improved guidance. SCOTFI, the trade association for timber frame suppliers in Scotland, has encouraged debate among its members.

The third step in the process is public information, debate, and education. Public attitudes will need to change if the majority of customers for houses in the countryside are to become interested in and want design quality before embarking on the planning process. Efforts to reach the public should be channelled through the media rather than through official publications. A good public relations initiative is needed, sponsored in the first instance perhaps by the Scottish planning authorities as an aspect of their design guidance work. Amenity groups could give useful advice. Magazines devoted to country living, the Sunday Supplements, and television (in programmes similar to the popular garden design programmes) should be used to reach a mass audience. Schools could raise awareness of the issues and promote informed discussion.

The fourth step is the promotion of competitions and awards leading to demonstration projects. These would allow a wide involvement of suppliers and house-builders, design professionals, amenity groups, the press and the public to become more aware of what can be done on the ground. The most practical form for these to take might be design-and-build competitions for small groups of new houses, designed as prototypes for individual providers, to be built speculatively for sale, either by themselves or as part of mixed-tenure schemes. Ideally there would be several such projects in different regions to bring out variations in local character. To attract interest from the industry and to encourage the development of new ranges, it would be helpful if funding agencies could under-write the sales of the completed developments. The Saltire Society Housing Awards panel has introduced a new category for new housing in rural areas of one or more dwellings. Previously the minimum entry was for a group of six houses. This may create the incentive for improved design submissions for Saltire Housing Awards. Several other awards for good design in the countryside have recently been promoted. Similar awards schemes should be encouraged.

The fifth step is advice directed to individual households embarking on the process of individual provision. Independent advice on procurement of design and constructional services might be brought within the scope of Scottish Homes's information and advice service. Professional bodies and trade associations could provide further advice. The RIAS's Directory of Practices is based on a database, updated every two years, which shows potential clients the skills and experience of architects' firms. The RIAS has said there would be little difficulty in adding information to the Directory to show skills and experience in these fields. The industry should be encouraged to set up an advisory service to potential customers on design and procurement. Examples of such advice centres attached to demonstration projects, sponsored by manufacturers and utilities companies, can be found in other countries. Information on designs, manufacturers, design services, components and fitments, and fuel and energy efficiency, is made available at these to members of the public, who can inspect built examples and who are given access to databases of information from suppliers. The timber frame industry, energy suppliers, and design professions should set up a similar centre, or, better still, several such centres, in Scotland.

A, high quality purpose designed, timber frame house under construction near Aviemore, in Badenoch and Strathspey. The house nestles comfortably into the sloping site. Walls are rough sawn cedar boarding and the low-pitched roof is clad in zinc sheeting. Rafters project over the walls to give generous roof overhangs, and are expressed internally. There are large windows facing south and west.

Several of these features — the low roof pitch, overhanging eaves and verges, window proportioning and general detailing — when they are found in suburban house types, are criticised for being out of character with traditional rural styles. Yet this house is obviously an example of imaginative and coherent architecture, carried off with conviction. It illustrates the point that design guidance can not easily be reduced to a set of simple rules, and that room needs to be left in the planning control process for the development of style.

In the countryside, the quality and form of the landscape can be the inspiration, not necessarily the character of houses that have been built in the past.

Architect :Roddy Langmuir
of Edward Cullinan Architects

REFERENCES

1   W. R. Lethaby. (1911). *Architecture.* London: Richard Clay & Sons.

2   D. Clapham, K. Kintrea, G. McAdam. Centre for Housing Research, University of Glasgow. (1991). *Individual Self Provision of Housing in Scotland.* Unpublished.

3   M. Shucksmith. (1990). *Housebuilding in Britain's Countryside.* London: Routledge.

4   D. Clapham, K. Kintrea, G. McAdam. Ibid.

5   B. P. Langrick. (1993). *New Rural Housing: Attitudes to Residential Developments in the Countryside.* University of Aberdeen and Robert Gordon's University. Unpublished Project.

6   Scottish Homes. (1990). *Rural Housing Market Studies - A Summary.* Research Report no. 13. Edinburgh: Scottish Homes.

7   B. P. Langrick. Ibid.

8   J. Andrews. (1990). The Challenge of Modern Housing on Skye. Unpublished.

9   D. Clapham, K. Kintrea, G. McAdam. Ibid.

10   D. Clapham, K. Kintrea, G. McAdam. Ibid.

11   RIAS. (1991). *RIAS/Wellgrove Timber Systems Ltd. Timber Frame Design Questionnaire Report.* Unpublished.

12   B. P. Langrick. Ibid.

13   D. Clapham, K. Kintrea, G. McAdam. Ibid.

14   Alasdair Alldridge. (1993) in *Fields of Vision: New Ideas in Rural Housing.* Edinburgh: RIAS.

15   Charles Mckean. (1993) in *Fields of Vision: New Ideas in Rural Housing.* Edinburgh: RIAS.

16   The section on history draws on R. J. Naismith's pioneer survey (1985) *Buildings of the Scottish Countryside.* London: Victor Gollancz for the Countryside Commission for Scotland.

17   A. Reiach, R. Hurd. (1944). *Building Scotland.* Edinburgh.

18   W. R. Lethaby. (1920). *Architecture as Form in Civilization.* OUP.

19   David Jarman. (1993) in *Fields of Vision: New Ideas in Rural Housing.* Edinburgh: RIAS.

20   The sections on where to build, and scale and overall form, draw on J. M. Fladmark, G. Y. Mulvagh and B. M. Evans. (1991). *Tomorrow's Architectural Heritage.* Edinburgh and London: Mainstream Publishing.

XV

C O M P A R A T I V E   N O T I O N A L   C O S T I N G S

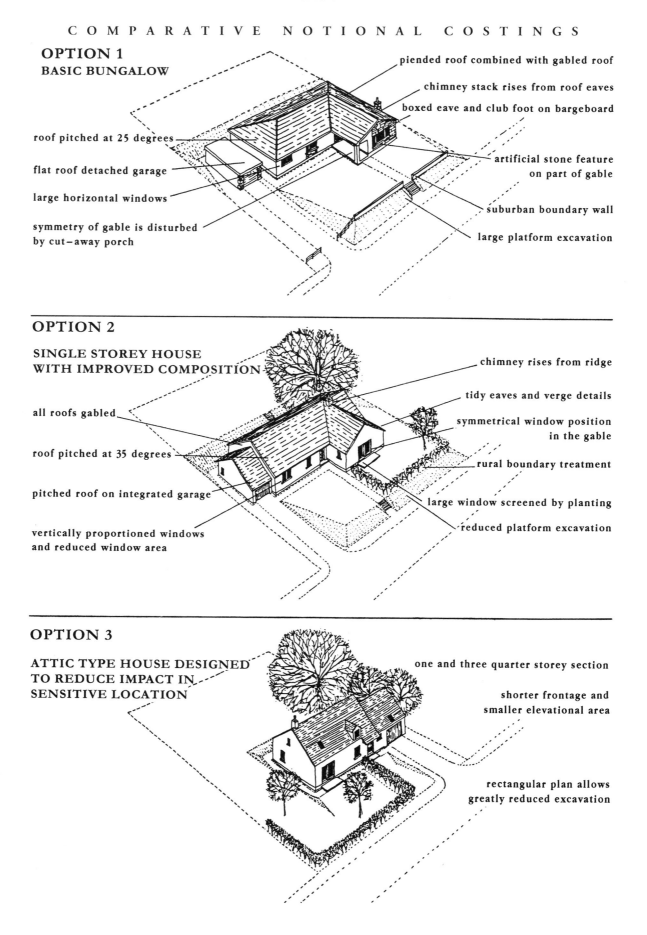

OPTION 1
BASIC BUNGALOW

piended roof combined with gabled roof

chimney stack rises from roof eaves

boxed eave and club foot on bargeboard

roof pitched at 25 degrees

flat roof detached garage

large horizontal windows

symmetry of gable is disturbed
by cut−away porch

artificial stone feature
on part of gable

suburban boundary wall

large platform excavation

OPTION 2

**SINGLE STOREY HOUSE
WITH IMPROVED COMPOSITION**

chimney rises from ridge

tidy eaves and verge details

symmetrical window position
in the gable

all roofs gabled

roof pitched at 35 degrees

pitched roof on integrated garage

vertically proportioned windows
and reduced window area

rural boundary treatment

large window screened by planting

reduced platform excavation

OPTION 3

**ATTIC TYPE HOUSE DESIGNED
TO REDUCE IMPACT IN
SENSITIVE LOCATION**

one and three quarter storey section

shorter frontage and
smaller elevational area

rectangular plan allows
greatly reduced excavation

OPTION 1

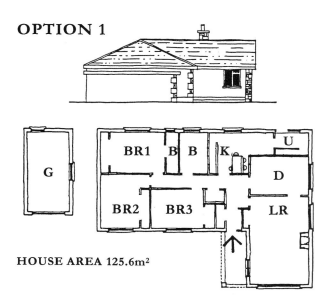

HOUSE AREA 125.6m²

OPTION 2

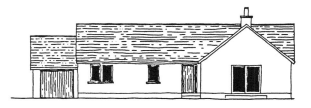

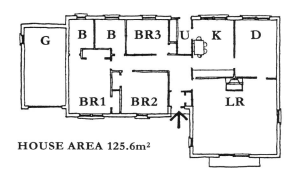

HOUSE AREA 125.6m²

By comparison with option 1:

EXTRA COSTS		SAVINGS	
Sub attic roof trusses and		Feature panel of artificial stone	
craneage. Stair. Chimney.		Reduced substructure	
Dormer. Structure		Reduced area of cladding	
House	+£3,925	House	-£3,950
Garage	+£1,500	Reduced excavation	-£ 900
	+£5,425	Savings	-£4,850
Savings	-£4,850		
Net extra cost	+ £575		

OPTION 3

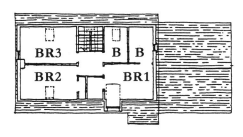

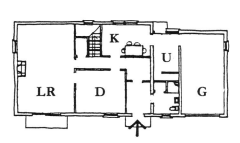

HOUSE AREA 125.6m²

By comparison with option 1:

EXTRA COSTS		SAVINGS	
Increased wall area		Feature panel of artificial stone	
Resulting from steeper roof		Reduced substructure	
House	+£1,255	House	-£ 850
Garage	+£1,000	Reduced excavation	-£ 275
	+£2,255	Savings	-£1,125
Savings	-£1,125		
Net extra cost	+£1,130		

The authors are architects. John Richards CBE, AA Dipl, D Univ, RSA, RIBA, PPRIAS, was for many years chairman of a large Edinburgh-based practice. He has been President of the Royal Incorporation of Architects in Scotland, and a member of the Royal Fine Art Commission in Scotland. He has been active in building research and architectural education, and has gained wide experience of social housing in Scotland as chairman of the Scottish Committee of the Housing Corporation and as Deputy Chairman of Scottish Homes. Margaret Richards RIBA, ARIAS, has specialised knowledge of architectural conservation. She has been a member of the Historic Buildings Council for Scotland and the National Committee of the Architectural Heritage Society for Scotland, and she is a member and a past chairman of Lothian Building Preservation Trust. John and Margaret Richards now practise in a small specialised architectural consultancy, based in a farming village in East Lothian

HMSO publications are available from:

HMSO Bookshops
71 Lothian Road, Edinburgh, EH3 9AZ
031-228 4181 Fax 031-229 2734
49 High Holborn, London, WC1V 6HB
071-873 0011 Fax 071-873 8200 (counter service only)
258 Broad Street, Birmingham, B1 2HE
021-643 3740 Fax 021-643 6510
33 Wine Street, Bristol, BS1 2BQ
0272 264306 Fax 0272 294515
9-21 Princess Street, Manchester, M60 8AS
061-834 7201 Fax 061-833 0634
16 Arthur Street, Belfast, BT1 4GD
0232 238451 Fax 0232 235401

HMSO Publications Centre
(Mail, fax and telephone orders only)
PO Box 276, London, SW8 5DT
Telephone orders 071-873 9090
General enquiries 071-873 0011
(queuing system in operation for both numbers)
Fax orders 071-873 8200

HMSO's Accredited Agents
(see Yellow Pages)

and through good booksellers

THE SCOTTISH OFFICE
Building Directorate

Printed in Scotland for HMSO by CCN° 13129   2/94 20M